A-Z
of the
80s

A-Z of the 80s

ALLY MOLLOY

JB

JOHN BLAKE

Published by John Blake Publishing Ltd,
3 Bramber Court, 2 Bramber Road,
London W14 9PB, England

www.johnblakebooks.com

www.facebook.com/johnblakebooks ⨍
twitter.com/jblakebooks ⨍

First published in paperback in 2017

ISBN: 978-1-84358-257-1

British Library Cataloguing-in-Publication Data:
A catalogue record for this book is available from the British Library.

Design by www.envydesign.co.uk

Printed in Great Britain by CPI Group (UK) Ltd

3 5 7 9 10 8 6 4 2

Text copyright © Ally Molloy, 2010

Papers used by John Blake Publishing are natural, recyclable products made from
wood grown in sustainable forests. The manufacturing processes conform to the
environmental regulations of the country of origin.

Introduction

Welcome to this A–Z guide to the 80s, that turbulent decade when the 'Iron Lady' Margaret Thatcher governed Britain, or at least the adult population – the young had other ideas about who their leaders were.

It was a roller-coaster time that saw riots in the streets and triumph in the creative powers of those who made music and films, wrote comedy, and designed fashion. Never before had the young had less in common with their parents' generation, or with those who belonged to a different tribe from the one they'd elected to join.

Goths, Casuals, Trendies, Mods and Skins were just some of the names adopted by the young in order to define their choice of lifestyle. Each tribe had its own fashions, vocabularies, and each pledged fierce allegiance to the bands they followed.

For the majority with jobs it was a decade of prosperity, and the age of electronic gadgetry was just about to take off with the first home computers and mobile telephones that were the size of house bricks.

In the past, class, education, and accent had divided Britain, but now the young decided their own pigeonholes. Snobbery was ignored and 'knowing your place' was a thing of the past. For the youth in the 80s, their place was the one they made for themselves. It was about a choice of lifestyle rather than a category decided on by social pressures. Nothing was the same any more… read all about it in this guide to the decade that changed everything.

ABC

Music journalist Martin Fry interviewed an obscure band for a fanzine in 1980 … and decided to quit his job and become their lead singer, forming ABC. Originally pigeon-holed as part of the New Romantic movement, the band were soon combining synthesizers with orchestras to produce a polished, brighter pop sound and their lyrics, often slanted towards unrequited love and heavy on the rhyming couplets, struck a chord with the pop loving nation. Following the release of 1982's number one album *Lexicon of Love*, ABC scored three top ten hits with 'Poison Arrow', 'The Look of Love' and 'All of My Heart'.

Other notable 80s bands scoring hit singles included New Wave Scots Aztec Camera and anti-fascist post-punkers Angelic Upstarts. Aneka had a one hit wonder with 'Japanese Boy' and Altered Images broke away from supporting Siouxsie and the Banshees to bring us 'Happy Birthday'.

Accused, The

This 1988 film told an extraordinarily powerful story with two magnificent performances by Kelly McGillis, as lawyer Kathryn Murphy, and Jodie Foster as rape victim, Sarah Tobias. Kelly McGillis, who had been raped in real life, was originally offered the part of the victim but she passed it to Jodie Foster who won the Oscar for her role. The premise of the movie is that Sarah cannot get justice because she is a rough, working class waitress who smokes dope and fools around with boys – the implication is that she got what she deserved. The three rapists are let off on a lesser charge but Sarah and Kathryn won't give up. The go for the spectators who stood by clapping and cheering and charge them with 'criminal solicitation'. The scene showing the rape in flashback is harrowing and at the same time heartbreaking. It was a fantastic job of directing by John Kaplan.

JODIE FOSTER

Acid House

They say if you can remember the 'second summer of love' then you weren't there – but at least we have a sea of smiley faces to remind us that 1988 was the year of Acid House. The in-crowd didn't go 'clubbing' any more, they 'raved' to a new style of electronic, repetitive and trance-like dance music. Followers insisted that the movement was about love, tolerance and equality and these haphazard gatherings often took place in fields, warehouses and vacant buildings. But landowners soon cashed in, charging exorbitant licence fees to stage the events, and the press condemned raves as hotbeds of hedonism and illegal drugs such as Ecstasy and LSD. This dance music revolution was forced out of the underground into the mainstream. Suddenly granddads were wearing smiley T-shirts and the movement lost its 'cool' reputation.

Adam and the Ants

In tight breeches, ruffled shirts and with inexplicable white stripes painted across their noses, this band of self-styled Dandy Highwaymen stormed into the mainstream British music scene in 1980 with the album *Kings of the Wild Frontier*. Lead singer Adam Ant was the alter ego of Stuart Goddard, a former art student. He was the driving force behind the band whose flamboyant mix of pirate fashion, pantomime pastiche and 18th-century historical lyrics gave the Ants a theatrical edge. A distinctive double drum beat, inspired by Native and African music, formed the foundation for their songs and they labelled this new kind of sound Antmusic. Their second album *Prince Charming* was their biggest hit with 'Stand and Deliver' and 'Prince Charming', backed up by tongue-in-cheek melodramatic and over-the-top videos, both reaching number one in the singles charts. No one ever really knew what the white stripes were for, but this was the 80s, so no one really cared!

Adverts

The 80s was a stellar decade for memorable TV adverts. The gorgeous Nick Kamen stripped down to his boxers in a launderette to sell Levi jeans. J.R. Hartley was looking for his Fly Fishing manual in the Yellow Pages, model Paula Hamilton threw away her pearls and dumped her mink coat in favour of a Volkswagen and we saw true love blossom over a cup of Gold Blend. The dancing skeleton rapping, 'Rerecord not fade away,' over a Chuck Berry riff sold millions of Scotch blank video tapes and a Venetian gondolier who warbled 'Just one Cornetto' so captured the public's imagination that Princess Diana was rumoured to have sung it to calm her nerves on her wedding day.

Aerobics

The craze for aerobics really took of in the 80s, as people became more health conscious and aware of the benefits of exercise. Programmes were created to be performed to music to combine rhythmic exercise with strength training routines and cardio-vascular fitness and classes began to take place in gymnasiums, hired halls or anywhere a group of like-minded people wanted to workout together under the eye of an instructor who encouraged them to 'feel the burn'.

A-ha

Legend has it that this Norwegian pop group were responsible for the ripped jeans fashion craze of 1985 after lead singer Morten Harket tore the front of his jeans on an amplifier whilst rushing on stage. Whether or not this tale is urban folklore, the truth is, A-ha became a teeny bop sensation and their synth pop ballads including 'Take On Me' and 'The Sun Always Shines on TV' sold more than 7 million copies worldwide. In their homeland they are considered close to royalty and they were chosen to write and perform the theme song for the 1987 James Bond film *The Living Daylights*. It is claimed that to achieve the same ripped jeans look in subsequent performances Harket used a razor blade. He could have just used his razor-sharp cheekbones!

AIDS

Although AIDS was first recognised by the US Centre for Disease Control and Prevention in 1981, the message was not really driven home in the UK until 1986, when the British government launched a major public information campaign with the slogan 'AIDS: Don't Die of Ignorance'. The haunting TV ads were narrated by John

Hurt and information leaflets were sent to every home in the country warning – 'Anyone can get it, gay or straight, male or female. Already 30,000 people are infected.' The disease had first hit the gay male community and had been initially dubbed: the 'gay plague' or 'gay cancer' and religious zealots claimed it was a sign from God. But soon it became apparent that the disease does not discriminate according to sexuality and the sexual liberation of the 60s and 70s was over. The late 80s saw huge rises in the sales of condoms and many television programmes openly began to discuss safe sex and soap operas and drama series incorporated the disease into their storylines.

Airplane!

This original spoof airport disaster movie was made in 1980, and with each viewing you will discover yet another set of brilliant jokes packed into its 86 minutes. It was written and directed by Jim Abrahams and brothers Jerry and David Zucker, who got the idea when they saw a dreadful 1957 disaster movie called *Zero Hour* on late-night TV. Clever casting thrust Lloyd Bridges and Leslie Nielsen, previously serious dramatic actors, into entirely new careers as comedians. The other players include Julie Hagerty as the air hostess who eventually has to help the passenger, Robert Hays, a traumatised veteran navy pilot, land the jumbo jet when the captain and the rest of the crew have succumbed to food poisoning. Even though a

RICHARD GIBSON
AS HERR FLICK IN
'ALLO 'ALLO

couple of the bad taste gags would never get onto the screen these days it is rightly considered a masterpiece of comedy

'Allo 'Allo

First broadcast in 1982, this show was the brainchild of David Croft, the man who gave viewers those other vintage comedies, *Hi-De-Hi* and *Are You being Served?* Co-written by Jeremy Lloyd, *'Allo 'Allo* ran for ten years and made national institutions of the characters that occupied the fictional French town of Nouvion during the years of German occupation. As a parody of the British post-war prisoner escape movies, the makers decided to reverse the usual formula and show the war from the side of the Resistance and the Germans. So, the unlikely hero was Gorden Kaye, playing René Artois, a tubby restaurateur, whose battleaxe of a wife, Edith, (Carmen Silvera) never suspects her bumbling husband of having a passionate but sexually frustrated affair with the saucy Yvette (Vicki Michelle). Other much loved characters included Officer Crabtree (Arthur Bostrom) an English spy posing as a gendarme whose absurd French accent led to mispronunciations like 'Good Moaning', Richard Marner as Colonel Von Strohm, Sam Kelly as Captain Hans Geering, Richard Gibson's memorable Gestapo agent, Herr Flick, Lieutenant Gruber (played by Guy Siner) and Michelle 'of the Resistance' Dubois (Kirsten Cooke) who repeats the immortal lines: 'Listen very carefully. I shall say this only once'. All contribute superbly to the well-balanced comedy team.

Almond, Marc

Forming one half of the synth pop duo Soft Cell, Almond topped the charts with his catchy electro-style cover of the obscure Northern Soul classic 'Tainted Love' in 1981. The radically reworked single broke all records as the track that remained the longest in the U.S billboard top 100 staying there for 43 weeks. Soft Cell were never afraid to break out of the mould of frothy, frivolous pop music and their album, *Non-Stop Erotic Cabaret*, which also featured the hits 'Bedsitter' and 'Sex Dwarf', became known for its dark lyrics which focused on the bleaker side of life including drugs, transvestism, murder and kinky sex. Although the band went on to record three more albums it is 'Tainted Love' that Almond is most remembered for, with Soft Cell's arrangement covered by the likes of Marilyn Manson and The Pussycat Dolls and sampled in Rihanna's 'SOS'.

Amadeus

A thoroughbred 1984 production brought from stage to screen by Milos Forman, who had Peter Shaffer write the script from his original play. The movie was showered

MARC ALMOND

with Academy Awards: Best Picture, Best Director, Best Actor, Best Screenplay, Best Art Direction, Best Costume Design, and Best Sound. The story tells of the destructive jealousy shown by rival Antonio Salieri towards the genius Wolfgang Amadeus Mozart. Salieri is both enchanted and bitterly wounded by the seemingly effortless talent displayed by the youthful Mozart. Hating himself for his own comparative lack of ability he sets about destroying the world renowned prodigy, who is, despite his awe inspiring music, still an immature childlike figure.

An American Werewolf in London

John Landis directed his cult classic horror movie in 1981 but he wrote it in the late sixties. The original idea came when he was on location in Yugoslavia for *Kelly's Heroes* and he saw a group of gypsies at a roadside performing a ritual to ensure one of their dead would not rise from in the grave. At first he had difficulties raising the finance because prospective backers thought the script was too funny to be a horror movie and too horrific to be a comedy. When he did raise the money, the producers wanted the leads to be played by Dan Aykroyd and James Belushi. Instead, Landis chose David Naughton and David Kessler with Jenny Agutter as the love interest. The story tells of two American friends being attacked on the Yorkshire moors by a werewolf. One is killed, the other wounded. Subsequently the dead companion returns from the grave to warn his surviving friend that he too has become a werewolf, and he must destroy himself before he begins a killing rampage. He does not heed the warning and tragedy ensues. One remarkable aspect of the film is the brilliant makeup of the werewolf, which won the movie an Oscar.

A MOVIE POSTER FOR *AN AMERICAN WEREWOLF IN LONDON*

An Officer and a Gentleman

This brilliant romantic drama of 1982 tells the tale of Zachary 'Zack' Mayo, played by Richard Gere, the motherless son of a rough US Navy boatswain's mate who signs on for Navy aviation officer training. There he clashes with Marine Gunnery Sergeant Emile Foley, played by Louis Gossett Jr., and also begins an affair with local working class girl, Paula, played by Debra Winger, who is on the lookout to marry an officer. The battles between the officer candidate and the Gunnery Sergeant give the movie plenty of tension; and his love life proves to be no easy passage either. But the Sergeant ultimately brings out the good in his charge and Zack passes out as a successful candidate. Whereupon, in a famous scene, he goes in his officer's whites to the factory where Paula works and sweeps her up in his arms to carry her off to a new life where she won't have to wear overalls anymore. Wonderfully sentimental stuff.

Arthur

Dudley Moore was nominated for an Academy Award for his part in this smash hit 1981 comedy, which was written and directed by Steve Gordon. Playing the title role of a drunken millionaire playboy, he starred opposite Liza Minnelli as the poor girl who wins his heart and John Gielgud, who received an Oscar for his part as Arthur's fatherly butler. The story is a modern-day fairy tale about the unhappy hero who is forced into an arranged marriage with an heiress he doesn't love so the two families preserve their fortunes. The most interesting aspect of the movie was the inspired chemistry between Dudley Moore and Liza Minnelli; they were utterly convincing as a couple who were meant to be together.

Astley, Rick

When his single 'Never Gonna Give You up' was released in 1987 everyone expected its creator to be a mature, traditional black soul singer. So when a 21-year-old pasty-

RICK ASTLEY

THE ATARI CONSOLE

faced, ginger-haired lad from Lancashire appeared on *Top of the Pops*, the country was stunned. Even more so that he performed the song while wearing a black polo neck and trench coat and dancing all with the grace of a *Thunderbirds* puppet. Nevertheless, the UK took Astley to their hearts, along with 16 other countries including most of Europe, Japan, Australia and the US, sending him straight to number one. He holds the record for being the only male solo artist to have his first eight singles reach the UK Top Ten. Astley had faded into obscurity by the early 1990s but in 2007 he became something of an internet phenomenon when 25 million internet users were tricked into watching a video of 'Never Gonna Give You Up' after it was posted under the name of other popular video titles. It was a practice that became known as 'Rickrolling'. In a tongue in cheek attempt to get in on the act YouTube pranked its viewers by making every single video on their front page on April Fools' Day in 2008 a Rickroll.

Atari

This home video-game console took us out of the arcades and made gaming possible in our own living rooms. Across the world millions of pundits became glued to their joysticks as they fought furious on-screen battles with *Space Invaders*, *Asteroids* and *Pac Man*. It may seem clunky and elementary in comparison to today's more sophisticated consoles but Atari was a massive break-through in its day and is widely seen as the godfather to its successors Sega and Nintendo.

A-Team, The

On the run from the military for a 'crime they didn't commit' these soldiers of fortune were everybody's favourite TV action men. Widely known for its cartoon-style portrayal of violence in which no one ever really got seriously hurt, the show was popular worldwide and crossed all generations. With its instantly recognisable theme tune and quirky, comic characters who possessed uncanny skills at making weapons and vehicles out of old parts, the show also attracted guest stars such as Boy George and Hulk Hogan, who were fans. The adventures centred on a group of United States ex-special forces who worked on the side of good and helped the oppressed. *The A-Team* ran for five years and starred George Peppard as Hannibal, Dirk Benedict as Faceman and Dwight Schultz as Capt 'Howling Mad' Murdock . The show also launched the career of Mr T, who played the most loved and well known character B.A. (Bad Attitude) Baracus and spawned the catchphrases 'I ain't getting on no plane' and 'I love it when a plan comes together.'

Bad Manners

Bad Manners was fronted by larger-than-life lead singer Buster Bloodvessel (real name Douglas Trendel). The ska revivalist band were most popular between 1980 and 1983 when they spent 111 weeks in the UK charts. Particularly successful songs were 'Lip Up Fatty', 'Lorraine' and 'My Girl Lollipop'.

Back to the Future

This movie, made in 1985, was the first of three adventures charting the time travelling exploits of Marty McFly and it got off to a bad start. To the dismay of the director, Robert

MICHAEL J. FOX AND
CHRISTOPHER LLOYD
TRAVEL THROUGH TIME
IN ONE OF THE BEST
LOVED FILMS OF THE 80S.

Zemeckis, he realised after the first month's shooting that he had cast the wrong actor in the lead role. So he fired Eric Stoltz and gave the part to Michael J. Fox, who was perfect, giving the role a defining charm. Even when he meets his as yet unmarried mother in the past and she feels a powerful attraction for him, Fox makes the encounters funny and avoids what could have been a toe-curling embarrassment for the audience. Marty McFly has arrived in 1956 by accident and his presence causes mayhem. Apart from prematurely inventing the skateboard, he must see to it that his mother and father kiss at their High School prom dance, thus ensuring their future marriage that will produce Marty and his brother and sister. The complicated plot moves at a breakneck pace and eventually all the pieces of various jigsaws fall into place.

Bananarama

This trio of Bristol-born art students were a mainstay of 1980s pop and dance music. Siobhan Fahey, Keren Woodward and Sara Dallin found initial success collaborating with vocal band Fun Boy Three on 1982 single 'T'aint What You Do (It's The Way That You Do It)'. They had their biggest chart success with the Stock Aitken and Waterman-produced 'Venus' in 1988. Known at first for their backcombed hair and baggy dungarees, they progressed from the girls-next-door look to become fashion icons and entered the higher echelons of pop with the most ever chart entries for an all-female group. The original line-up changed when Siobhan left the band and went on to marry Eurhythmics guitarist Dave Stewart.

Band Aid

The original fund raising super group was born in 1984 to Bob Geldof and Midge Ure as a way to bring relief to famine-struck Ethiopia. The single 'Do They Know It's Christmas', features a plethora of 80s rock and pop royalty, became the biggest selling single in UK chart history and sold a staggering 12.5m worldwide. Recorded on a freezing November day, thanks to Geldof's clever PR, the world's press watched as stars such as Duran Duran, U2, George Michael and The Style Council arrived at producer Trevor Horn's SARM West recording studio in London's Notting Hill.

Basil, Toni

Antonia Christina Basilotta, who was born on 22 September 1943, is best known for her 1982 worldwide smash hit, 'Mickey'. Her punk cheer leader style and energetic dance routine made her a favourite with teenage girls. Basil began her career as a choreographer and incorporated her expertise into the iconic dance routine featured in the 'Mickey' video. Both Madonna and Kylie Minogue later covered the song.

Batman

In 1939 a new hero made his debut in Detective Comics when Batman first hit the page. First filmed cheaply in the 40s, it was reintroduced later in a camp version for television and in 1989 it was brought to the cinema screen again, but this time with a big budget, and Michael Keaton in the lead role. He hadn't been first choice for the part; the makers had wanted Mel Gibson but he wasn't

BATMAN

available. With its bizarrely inventive villains, wonderful Oscar-winning Art Deco sets of Gotham City, and the new hi-tech equipment used by the hero, the dark crusader had finally come into his own. The film is a slickly-told story of how millionaire orphan Bruce Wayne creates a character that will strike terror into the hearts of criminals as an act of vengeance for his parents who were slain in a robbery.

Baywatch

The most-watched TV show of all time, *Baywatch* burst onto our screens in 1989. The show centred around the lives, loves and adventures of a team of Californian lifeguards, and starred David Hasselhoff as team leader Mitch Buchannon and featured gorgeous Playboy model Erica Eleniak as the first nubile, tanned lady lifeguard to run in slow motion whilst wearing the now notorious red swimsuit.

Berlin Wall

At the end of World War II the city of Berlin, which lay in the communist zone of East Germany, had been divided between east and west, but access between the two zones had been unhampered. But by 1961 so many people were seeking refuge in West Berlin that the East German government, encouraged by the Russians, built the Berlin

DAVID HASSELHOFF IN THE FAMOUS RED SHORTS.

Wall to seal in the East German population, a provocative act that caused much political and social unrest. By 1989, there was enormous pressure from the East German people and the fall of the 81-mile wall became inevitable.

During a 1987 speech at Berlin's Brandenburg Gate commemorating the 750th anniversary of the city, US President Ronald Reagan challenged General Secretary of the Soviet Communist Party, Mikhail Gorbachev to 'Tear down this wall'. Two years later, on 9 November 1989, the wall fell as people attacked the hated symbol of oppression with their bare hands. Finally, it was demolished completely in the following weeks as the world watched and cheered.

Best Selling Books of the 80s

1980: *The Bourne Identity* by Robert Ludlam, *Princess Daisy* by Judith Krantz, *Fire Starter* by Stephen King.

1981: *The Hotel New Hampshire* by John Irving, *Gorky Park* by Martin Cruz Smith.

1982: *Mistral's Daughter* by Judith Krantz, *Jane Fonda's Workout Book* by Jane Fonda, *No Bad Dogs* by Barbara Woodhouse.

1983: *The Name of the Rose* by Umberto Eco.

1984: *The Sicilian* by Mario Puzo, *The Fourth Protocol* by Fredrick Forsyth.

1985: *Dancing in the Light* by Shirley MacLaine, *Secrets* by Danielle Steel.

1986: *Hollywood Husbands* by Jackie Collins.

1987: *Misery* by Stephen King.

1988: *To Be the Best* by Barbara Taylor Bradford.

1989: *The Satanic Verses* by Salman Rushdie.

Beverly Hills Cop

Nothing defines Hollywood as the heart of the movie 'industry' better than films like this 1984 smash hit: an original dramatic plot existed that was considered in turn by both Al Pacino and Sylvester Stallone before it was reworked as a star making comedy drama for Eddie Murphy. The necessary craftsmen were put to work and what they manufactured was a brilliantly successful role for Murphy as the unorthodox Detroit policeman, Axel Foley, who takes leave to pursue the killers of his partner to Beverly Hills. There he encounters two strictly by-the-book cops played by Judge Reinhold and John Ashton, who are appalled by Murphy playing fast and loose with the law in order to get his man. Not a profound movie, but a fine example of Hollywood polish. As the song says, 'That's Entertainment.'

Blues Brothers, The

Like many cult movies, *The Blues Brothers* was not a big hit when it was released in 1980. Written by Dan Aykroyd and John Landis, who also directed the movie, it was a spin off from the television show *Saturday Night Live*. Apart from Aykroyd's co-star, John Belushi, the film was packed with stars from the world of American soul and rhythm and blues, but this was time when the kids of America were keener on pop music. Still the supporting cast list is impressive. Watch out for Carrie

THE *BLUES BROTHERS'* SIGNATURE POSE

Fisher, Twiggy, Bill Murray, Ray Charles, Cab Calloway and John Candy. The plot has Dan Aykroyd and John Belushi dressed in matching pork pie hats, sun glasses and tight black suits 'On a mission from God,' to raise money to save their old orphanage by reuniting their old blues band to play a charity gig. Anarchic chaos follows, with spectacular results.

BMX bikes

The craze for riding BMX bikes has its origins in California in the 60s when kids began using bikes to imitate motocross, the sport performed on motorcycles. Hence, BMX stood for 'bike motocross'.

The sport really took off in the 80s and swept the world, with more and more manufacturers developing specialised and expensive bikes for the new legions of devotees.

Blackadder

When the first series of *Blackadder* was shown in 1983 it was not an immediate success. Written by Rowan Atkinson and Richard Curtis, the central character (also played by Atkinson) was rather like a medieval Mr Bean. But once Atkinson signed over his job as co-writer to Ben Elton, the show found its feet. Instead of a face-pulling nerd, the character of Blackadder evolved to become a sharp, cynical coward, dealing disdainfully down the ages

ROBBIE COLTRANE AND ROWAN ATKINSON LAUGH IT UP IN *BLACKADDER*.

with the selfish vanities of his superiors and the invincible stupidities of his hereditary working-class servant, Baldrick. Rowan Atkinson was superb and so were the brilliant cast of supporting players. Once seen, Miranda Richardson's portrayal of a psychopathic Elizabeth I is never to be forgotten. Stephen Fry and Hugh Laurie contributed magnificently to the fun and there were delightful occasional appearances by Rik Mayall. Despite the brilliance of the humour, the last scene of the final episode was deeply moving. Set in the trenches of World War I, Blackadder can no longer avoid the battle, and is finally shown advancing to his inevitable death against the enemy machine guns.

Black Monday

Starting in Hong Kong and spreading west through international time zones, 19 October 1987 saw the world's stock markets crash, finally leading to the Dow Jones Industrial Average dropping a staggering 508 points.

The increasing panic led to £50 billion being wiped off shares in the London Stock Exchange. Until then, the 80s was a decade of extravagance and opulence, with City workers notorious for their decadent spending habits. Faced with a financial reality check, the era that started with such buoyant optimism was suddenly heading for recession.

Blade Runner

Based on Philip K Dick's 1968 novel *Do Androids Dream Of Electric Sheep?* this iconic movie suffered worse than expected ticket sales, but since then *Blade Runner* has achieved a richly deserved reputation as one of the greatest science fiction movies of all time. Ridley Scott's epic was set in a dystopian Los Angeles and starred Harrison Ford, Rutger Hauer, Darryl Hannah and Sean Young as the humanoid replicants/robots and the blade runner/bounty hunter out to 'retire' them. The movies main themes regarding the nature of love and indeed humanity itself were summed up in Dutch actor Hauer's famously ad-libbed soliloquy but the theme was counter balanced by awesome sets and acrobatic fight scenes.

Blitz Club

Based in London's Covent Garden, the Blitz was the brainchild of flatmates Steve Strange and Rusty Egan, who would later find fame as Visage. With Egan as DJ and Strange running a strict door policy regarding the dress code – only the most flamboyant and theatrically attired were allowed entrance – the club was birthplace for the New Romantic movement (*see* Youth Tribes). Regulars, known as 'Blitz Kids', included Boy George, Midge Ure, the then-unsigned Spandau Ballet, Depeche Mode, Marilyn and Pete Burns of Dead or Alive. Mick Jagger was famously refused entry for lacking the requisite image.

Blockbusters

Presented by actor Bob Holness, this quiz show came to the UK from America in 1983 and gained a cult following among the sixth-form students from whom it drew its contestants. The formula had a game board of hexagons on which the contestants charted a path across or down by answering trivia questions. Winners could gain prizes for themselves or their colleges. As a trained actor, Bob Holness assumed the role of a genial stick-in-the-mud, a persona that worked well and actually endeared him to his audience. Part of the following came from sly attempts at getting gently 'improper' sayings into the show, after the infamous line 'Can I have a "P" please, Bob?' was heard on air.

Bonfire of the Vanities

Summing up the very worst aspects of the decade, Tom Wolfe's novel and the movie adaptation which followed are widely regarded as the definitive depiction of the vain, self-centred, money-orientated essence of 1980s New York City.

Ambition, racism, class politics and greed are central to the story of Sherman McCoy, a white, millionaire city bond trader who, along with his mistress, is involved in a hit and run accident in which a black teenager is injured.

The movie, though a critical and commercial flop, is now seen as one of the definitive 80s films and starred Tom Hanks, Melanie Griffith and Bruce Willis.

Boris Becker

In 1985, at just 17 years of age, Boris Becker became the youngest ever Wimbledon champion. He was, in fact, a whole year younger than that year's junior champion. Whilst critics denounced this extraordinary achievement as a fluke, the teenage tennis protégé proved them all wrong by returning the following year and doing it all over again. Now known mostly for his turbulent private life, including fathering a child during a brief encounter at a top London restaurant, Boris Becker will forever be the 80s golden boy of the tennis court.

Boy George and Culture Club

Everyone's favourite gender-bender, Boy George (born George O'Dowd) exploded into the mainstream in late 1982 during his first *Top of the Pops* appearance with his band, Culture Club. Though they had failed to attract any attention with their first two releases, the third single from album *Kissing To Be Clever*, 'Do You Really Want To Hurt Me?' was an international smash hit and reached number two in the US charts. The band went on to even greater acclaim on the release of their second album, *Colour By Numbers*, when 'Church of The Poison Mind' reached the top 10 on both side of the Atlantic.

With 'Karma Chameleon', Culture Club achieved a number one hit in 16 countries and it eventually became one of the 20 best selling singles of the decade.

BOY GEORGE

With success came the dark side of fame. Amid rumours of drug addiction, and after several shambolic stage performances, George's younger brother David publicly claimed that George was seriously hooked on heroin, that his weight had plummeted by 56lbs, and that the family were waiting for a phone call telling them that George had been found dead from an overdose.

The press that had once courted him actively turned on him and he found himself the target of a tabloid frenzy, this time calling for his punishment.

More drama followed when 27-year-old musician and close friend of Boy George, Michael Rudetsky, died of a heroin overdose at the singer's London home.

Despite these tragic events, Boy George went on to beat heroin addiction. Though he later found some success as a club DJ, his career has never hit the same dizzy heights as in his 1980s heyday.

Brat Pack, The

Starring in a clutch of teen/coming of age movies, the Brat Pack consisted of the hippest, most precocious of Hollywood's young actors. Emilio Estevez, Rob Lowe, Andrew McCarthy, Antony Michael Hall, Demi Moore, Molly Ringwald, Judd Nelson, Ally Sheedy, John Cusack and Matthew Broderick all shone in films with highly successful, though slightly interchangeable, plotlines. The most successful, *Pretty in Pink*, *St Elmo's Fire*, *The Breakfast*

Club, *Class* and *Ferris Bueller's Day Off* have now achieved cult status. Some of the members went on to have highly lucrative careers in more adult-centred movies and some did not, though all have continued to stay in the public eye as the years have passed.

Bread

Written by Carla Lane, this highly successful comedy series, first aired in 1986, was about people at the bottom of society. Set in the Liverpool district of Dingle, *Bread* charted the ups and downs of the devoutly Roman Catholic Boswell family, headed by a matriarch called Nellie, played by Jean Boht. Although separated from her husband, the feckless Freddie (played by Ronald Forfar), Nellie still held him in deep affection, despite his having found a new partner called Lilo Lil (Eileen Pollock). The theme of the show was how the large family coped in Thatcher's Britain with only their welfare benefits and the proceeds from selling stolen goods.

Brighton Bomb

At 2.45 am on October 12 1984, a bomb planted weeks earlier by the IRA blasted four floors out of the Grand Hotel, Brighton. At the time the Grand Hotel was the residence and headquarters of the Tory leadership during the Conservative Party conference, so it was a miracle that the entire government of Great Britain and Northern Ireland wasn't wiped out by the blast. One Conservative MP, Sir Anthony Berry, and the wife of the government Chief Whip, John Wakeham, were killed and more than thirty people injured. Mr and Mrs Norman Tebbit were pulled badly injured from the wreckage and Margaret Thatcher, the Prime Minister, came within a hair's breadth of being killed, but she survived uninjured. Later she was quoted as saying, 'Life must go on.'

Brixton Riots

Throughout the early 1980s there were several riots in Britain, the most violent and destructive of which being the Brixton Riot of 11 April 1981, where almost 300 police and dozens of civilians were injured. Several premises were burned and 82 arrests were made. Damage to vehicles and looting were widespread.

Later, the Scarman Report, ordered by the then Home Secretary, Willie Whitelaw, found unquestionable evidence of disproportionate and indiscriminate use of 'stop and search' powers by the police against black people and that this was one of the major contributing factors.

Throughout the year there were other riots and lesser pockets of social disorder in Handsworth, Southall, Toxteth, Moss Side, Leeds, Leicester, Southampton, Halifax, Bedford, Gloucester, Coventry, Bristol and

Edinburgh. On 13 April, Mrs Thatcher dismissed the suggestion that unemployment and racial discrimination had caused the Brixton Riot, saying 'Nothing, but nothing justifies what happened.'

Bros

The gorgeous blond Goss twins Matt and Luke, along with Craig Logan, were the teen sensations of the late 1980s. They weren't particularly talented musicians, but they still attracted an army of teenage fans – known as the Brosettes – who sported a uniform of ripped Levi's 501 jeans and Doc Marten boots, with the inexplicable Bros addition of Grolsch bottle tops to the laces! Despite disappearing into obscurity by 1990, they are still known for their formulaic, best selling record 'When Will I Be Famous?'

Bucks Fizz

The fizzy blonde foursome was formed to deliver the United Kingdom's entry to the 1981 Eurovision Song Contest. The single, 'Making Your Mind Up', not only beat Germany to first place but went to number one in six countries, no doubt helped by the raunchy dance routine in which Mike Nolan and Bobby G ripped Cheryl Baker and Jay Aston's skirts off, leaving them in the briefest of minis. There was drama in 1984 when the

BUCKS FIZZ
PERFORMING.

band's tour bus crashed, leaving the singers with serious injuries, though all recovered eventually. More sensationally, the following summer saw Aston quit while still under contract amidst confessions that she had conducted an affair with Andy Hill, the husband of the band's creator, Nichola Martin.

Aston sold her story to a tabloid, shattering the band's cheerful, bubbly image with tales of in-house bitching. The group struggled on with Jay's replacement Shelley Preston, eventually changing record labels and line-ups again and again.

Bullseye

Launched in 1981, the half-hour show eventually became so popular when it was moved to its Saturday slot that it attracted fifteen million viewers every week. Hosted by genial Jim Bowen, who had started out in life as a teacher and became deputy head of a Lancashire school before turning to a new career in television, the format was straightforward: three pairs of contestants were each divided into dart thrower and question answerer. The formula was a crowd-pleaser, not least for the quality of the questions and Jim Bowen's blizzard of catch phrases.

Buzzwords

ADULT CHILD: Common term to describe the grown-up children of alcoholic and drug addict parents.

AIRHEAD: Usually applied to females who have no thoughts, apart from those concerning their personal appearance, in their brains.

BARF BAG: Lightweight insult for those girls who avoid anything too earthy in life.

BODACIOUS: Exclamation of approval for an attractive girl, usually by dumb surfer boys.

BOY TOY: A Madonna invention that originally meant a girl who was a toy for boys, but came to mean a boy that was used by an older woman or man.

CHILL OUT. To relax and face the world with calm detachment.

COUCH POTATO: Someone who spends the greater part of their lives watching television from the comfort of the sofa.

DIPSTICK: A mild form of abuse used to denote someone slow on the uptake.

DO LUNCH: 'We must do lunch together' became a popular way of saying a polite goodbye to someone with whom you actually had no intention of sharing a meal.

PHAT: A rapper word of approval for a woman who had sexy qualities.

SPACE CADET: Yet another way of saying someone was stupid.

SUCKS: Originally an anti-gay phrase, the term quickly lost its original connotation and moved into mainstream usage as a simple term of disapproval.

WICKED: A general term of approval that could be applied without discrimination to anything pleasurable or impressive.

YUPPIES: Said to be the acronym for 'young upwardly mobile professionals'. The word quickly became a term of abuse by poor people towards invaders who were gentrifying their neighbourhood.

Cabbage Patch Kids

The squashy-faced dolls were so in demand that some parents engaged in near riots when stores sold out. Created by folk artist Xavier Roberts, the original handmade dolls were sold at craft fairs around the United States. With both European and African-American versions available, the unique selling point was the little birth certificate and adoption paper that accompanied each doll, and a claim that no two dolls were ever alike.

Taken over by Coleco in 1982, the by now mass-produced toy was 16 inches long with a huge, vinyl head. The 1983 Christmas season heralded Cabbage Patch Kid frenzy and saw Coleco suspending all advertising after reports that a fruitless eight-hour wait for dolls had ignited such fury that a rioting crowd broke a woman's leg and forced a shop manager to defend himself with a baseball bat!

Captain Sensible

Co-founder of 70s band The Damned, Captain Sensible, aka Raymond Burns, burst on to the 80s pop scene with his cover of the Rodgers and Hammerstein *South Pacific* number, 'Happy Talk'. Wearing his signature red beret, Captain Sensible cheerily entertained us on *Top of The Pops* backed by the all-girl band Dolly Mixture. He later attracted slight controversy on the release of his anti-Falklands war song, 'Glad It's All Over' and his diatribe against the commercialisation of Christmas with 'One Christmas Catalogue'.

Care Bears

Originally characters created for use on birthday cards, these lovable images were turned into plush, 13-inch teddy bears and animated for two kids TV series, *The Care Bears* and *The Care Bears Family*. 1983's must-have toys were mostly identical in appearance with the exception of Good Luck Bear, who was winking, sleepy-looking Bedtime Bear and Grumpy Bear, who never cracked a smile.

Carlisle, Belinda

Achieving initial renown as the hefty, drug-taking lead singer with all girl new wave band The Go Gos, Carlisle metamorphosed in 1985 as a newly slim, narcotic-free solo star. Her undoubtedly beautiful face gracing a thousand magazine covers and her distinctive warbling falsetto throatily proclaiming 'Heaven Is A Place on Earth' is ingrained in many memories as a romantic first date song.

Chapman, Tracey

The multi-platinum selling Grammy-winning singer-songwriter is best known for singles such as 'Fast Car' and 'Baby Can I Hold You'. Holding degrees in Anthropology and African Studies, Chapman began street performing in Harvard Square and different coffee houses in Cambridge, Massachusetts and was signed to Elektra Records in 1987. Her first album, *Tracy Chapman*, was released to worldwide critical acclaim. She performed at the 1988 celebration for Nelson Mandela's 70th birthday and in the Amnesty International Human Rights Now! tour.

Chariots of Fire

The 1981 masterpiece cleaned up at that year's Academy Awards where, on accepting his statuette for Best Original

ALLY MOLLOY

BELINDA CARLISLE

Screenplay, Colin Welland famously announced: 'The British Are Coming'. Based on the story of Eric Liddell and Harold Abrahams, the British Gold medallists at the 1924 Olympics, the movie won a further six Oscars including Best Supporting Actor (Ian Holm) and Best Director (Hugh Hudson) best picture (producer David Putnam) as well as Film Editing, Costume Design and Original Music Score to composer Vangelis for his haunting theme and incidental music. The meticulously researched, superbly acted *Chariots of Fire* also featured a credit to Dodi Fayed, who was later to die in a car accident alongside Princess Diana, as executive producer.

Cheggers Plays Pop

Keith Chegwin, always known as Cheggers, was one of the star performers of 80s children's television. As well as a regular appearance on *Swap Shop* he hosted *Cheggers Plays Pop*, which was filmed at the BBC in Manchester and the schools from which it drew its contestants were mostly in the north and north-west of Britain, but its audience was truly national. Cheggers was a big name in Bristol as well as Barnsley.

As well as featuring contemporary pop groups performing in the studio there was also a contest between two teams of children representing their schools in which they had to compete both physically and mentally for the prizes.

Cher

Following a successful career as one half of 1960s duo Sonny and Cher, by 1980 Cher's career was at something of a standstill. Never one to be bogged down by failure, she bounced back, this time reinventing herself as an actress. Earlier forays into film had met with little success, but following a critically acclaimed performance on Broadway in *Come Back to the Five and Dime, Jimmy Dean, Jimmy Dean*, she was later cast in the movie version by director Robert Altman and duly received a Golden Globe for her performance. A year later, playing a lesbian, blue-collar worker opposite Meryl Streep in movie *Silkwood*, she received her first Academy Award nomination, eventually winning Best Actress in 1987 acting opposite Nicolas Cage, in *Moonstruck*. The same year she managed to revive her music career with the release of the highly successful album *Cher*, launched her own perfume called 'Uninhibited' and appeared in a number of her signature barely-there outfits. 1989 saw the release of 4.5 million-selling 'Heart of Stone' and her status as a gay icon was truly cemented.

CND

The replacement of Polaris with Trident missiles for the UK's submarine fleet, together with the deployment of American Pershing Missiles in Western Europe and the

CHER AND MICHAEL
JACKSON, TWO 80S ICONS

opposing SS20s in the Soviet Union, saw the Campaign for Nuclear Disarmament (CND) grow from 1979's membership of 4000 to a staggering 100,000 by 1984. Networks of members harassed missile convoys whenever they were moved by public road until the missiles were only transported at night and by police guard. A London demonstration in 1981 attracted 250,000 protestors and in 1983, three million people joined simultaneous protests across Europe making the peace movement of the 1980s the largest of the modern age.

Cocteau Twins

Alternative Scots band the Cocteau Twins were known primarily for their beautifully atmospheric vocals and their style was dubbed 'dream pop'. Their debut number, 'Garlands', was an immediate success on the alternative scene, as was their follow-up EP 'Lullabies'.

Collins, Phil

Following a bitter marital break-up, Genesis drummer Phil Collins re-emerged as a songwriting talent with his best selling 1981 album *Face Value*. Teaming up with Bob Geldof and Midge Ure to play drums on the 1984 Band Aid single 'Do They Know It's Christmas?', Collins went on to win more acclaim with following albums *Hello, I Must Be Going* and *No Jacket Required*, though he faced

PHIL COLLINS (*LEFT*) AND GENESIS.

some critical accusations of conforming to mainstream musical safety.

In 1985 he became the only artist to perform on both sides of the Atlantic at Live Aid, when he played in London and then Philadelphia after travelling to the US by Concorde.

In 1988, the former child star of the London stage (he had once played the Artful Dodger in a West End production of *Oliver*), Collins returned to acting. He appeared alongside Julie Walters in the hit movie *Buster*, the film version of the life of Great Train Robber Buster Edwards.

Color Purple, The

Filmed in 1985 from Alice Walker's Pulitzer prize-winning novel, it took a brave man in the shape of Steven Spielberg to take on this controversial project. The movie examined the life of Celie, an abused black girl in the rural southern states of America in the early part of the twentieth century. Although it launched Whoopi Goldberg, Danny Glover and Oprah Winfrey into stardom, the movie engendered a lot of hostility from black pressure groups. They objected to the unsympathetic portrayal of some of the African-American characters. Lesbian pressure groups also complained that the storyline in the book which examined the lesbian relationship that Celie has with her cruel husband's mistress had been suppressed. Although it was nominated for thirteen Oscars it won nothing and most critics consider the movie ultimately flawed.

Comic Strip Presents..., The

Making its debut with the launch of Channel 4 in 1982 the Comic Strip finally reached a mass audience with a series of sketches each heralded as *The Comic Strip*

Presents... The name Comic Strip first came to notice representing a group of brilliant young writers and performers who had made their mark performing before live audiences in London's club land. Originally at the Comedy Store, Rik Mayall and Adrian Edmondson, Nigel Planer and Peter Richardson and Dawn French and Jennifer Saunders set up their own show at the Raymond Revuebar, the famous Soho strip club. As founder, Peter Richardson had the other members sign contracts binding them to the new group.

With their growing success they came to the notice of Jeremy Isaacs, the head of Channel 4, and Peter Richardson negotiated a contract to sign up the group. Other new wave comedians flocked to the standard of the *Comic Strip Presents...* including Phil Cornwell, Al Pillay, Alexei Sayle, Robbie Coltrane, and Keith Allen.

Communards, The

Headed by falsetto-voiced Scottish songwriter Jimmy Somerville, the Communards had hits with covers of Thelma Huston's 'Don't Leave Me This Way' (the biggest selling British record of 1986) and the Jackson 5's 'Never Can Say Goodbye'. Previously front man for band Bronski Beat, Somerville teamed up with classically trained clarinet player Richard Coles and bassist Dave Renwick to form The Communards. After disbanding in 1988, Somerville went on to a solo career, whilst Coles was ordained into the Church of England and is now Chaplain to the Royal College of Music.

Compact Discs

To a world used to easily scratched vinyl or snapped cassette tapes, the compact disc was seen as a miracle of audio-technology. It was first presented to the UK public in 1981, via BBC technology show, *Tomorrow's World*, where it was thrown around the studio and smothered in jam!

Originally produced to store sound recordings, the idea was that a laser would read a pattern embedded in the disc and eliminate any scratchy sound produced by vinyl records. When Sony, CBS, Phillips and Polygram released a joint statement announcing the development of the first domestic CD system the idea moved from the realms of science fiction to reality. First available in Japan in 1982, they were then sold to the rest of the world the following year. The $1000 price tags meant that they were owned only by a select few and just as with the first video films, a very limited selection of titles were obtainable. These included Michael Jackson's *Thriller*, Billy Joel's *The Stranger* and Pink Floyd's *Wish You Were Here*. A sceptical press happily reported tiny sales figures in the first year of mainstream availability but lowering prices and a hugely expanded catalogue of titles meant that 20 million CDs had sold in America by the end of 1985.

Crocodile Dundee

Paul Hogan brought a great deal of easy charm to his role of Mick Dundee in this 1986 comedy thriller, which became a massive hit in America. Only using the nickname 'Crocodile' for the sake of tourists to the outback, Mick is a friend to all men including the native aborigines. After saving her life he is taken up by an American female reporter who persuades him to return to New York with her. There he deals with the big city jungle just as confidently as he does the inherent dangers of the Australian bush. His love affair with the girl takes a bit longer to ripen, but Mick prevails in the end.

Cruise, Tom

Despite being somewhat on the short side, Thomas Cruise Mapother IV, otherwise known as Tom Cruise, is considered by the top players of Tinsel Town to be one of the giants of Hollywood. His list of hit movies is impressive: *Risky Business*, *Top Gun*, *Days of Thunder*, *Minority Report*, *Rain Man*, and the three *Mission: Impossible* movies are all down to him. Less well known by the general public is just how highly he is regarded as a producer, who seems to be able to guarantee hit movies. Married three times, most famously to his second wife Nicole Kidman, he is a devoted supporter of the Church of Scientology, a religion founded by science fiction writer Ron Hubbard, who claimed human beings are descended from alien visitors from other planets.

TOM CRUISE IN *TOP GUN*

Dallas

This soap opera sensation centred on the oil-rich Ewing family, a bunch of Texan millionaires who all lived together at Southfork Ranch. The show was best known for its storylines of wealth, sibling rivalry, extra-marital affairs, scheming power struggles and for its cliffhangers. The main characters were JR, a greedy and ambitious oil baron, his better looking and kinder brother Bobby, their mother Miss Ellie, JR's alcoholic wife Sue Ellen, Bobby's beautiful wife Pam, their scheming sexpot niece Lucy and JR's arch rival Cliff Barnes. In 1980 an estimated 83 million viewers worldwide watched JR being shot in his office by an unknown assailant, generating the biggest

THE CAST OF *DALLAS*.

whodunnit storyline in television history. As fans waited with bated breath for six months to see who had pulled the trigger, 'Who Shot JR?' became the catchphrase of the year and was printed onto T-shirts, mugs, posters and bumper stickers which quickly sold out. The episode revealing the identity of the potential killer was aired first in America but as the storyline had so captured the world's attention, ITN's *New At Ten* revealed that night that JR had been shot by his sister-in-law and lover Kirstin.

Deaths

We said goodbye to some of the world's most beloved stars in the 1980s, including:

1980: John Lennon

1981: Natalie Wood

1982: Princess Grace of Monaco, Henry Fonda and John Belushi

1983: Muddy Waters, Karen Carpenter and David Niven

1984: Marvin Gaye and Diana Dors

1985: Orson Welles and Rock Hudson

1986: Cary Grant

1987: Fred Astaire, Andy Warhol and Liberace

1988: Frank Sinatra and Roy Rogers

1989: Bette Davis and Jimmy Cagney

Depeche Mode

Hailed by many as the most popular electronic band in history, this bunch of Essex boys who formed in 1980 have sold more than 100 million records worldwide and have had a staggering 48 songs in the UK singles chart, including the classics 'Just Can't Get Enough' and 'Everything Counts'. Later groups such as the Pet Shop Boys, A-ha, the Fear Factory and even singer Shakira credit Depeche Mode as a huge inspiration for their own music and many claim they were the pioneers of the techno music revolution that followed.

Diana, Princess of Wales

She is without doubt the most famous and iconic figure of the decade. We were first introduced to Lady Diana Spencer, the shy, 19-year-old nursery school assistant, in 1981 and she was immediately dubbed 'Lady Di' by the world's media. By the end of the decade Princess Diana had metamorphosed into the most photographed and fêted woman in the world. As the we watched her supposedly fairytale marriage to Prince Charles unfold from afar, Diana was facing demons behind closed palace doors in the shape of the eating disorder bulimia and her belief that her husband was having an affair. After giving birth to Princes William and Harry in 1982 and 1984 respectively, she used her own feelings of insecurity and inadequacy to fuel a compassion for the world's underdogs. By embracing India's 'untouchables', cradling sick babies and holding hands with dying Aids patients, Diana touched the world and created a new,

14ᴾ

29 July 1981

DIANA, PRINCESS OF WALES AND PRINCE CHARLES ON A
COMMEMORATIVE STAMP.

modern kind of royal, whom she insisted was not out of touch with the problems of the world. It was her very essence of normality that made Diana so beloved. Beautiful, and with an enviable figure, she was also a fashion icon – designers clamoured to dress her and the public imitated her sense of style. She was an 80s woman through and through and proved this by rollerblading around the vast halls of Kensington Palace, bopping in the audience at Duran Duran concerts and dancing on stage with Wayne Sleep. Throughout her life the public's appetite for all things Diana was never satisfied and her tragic death in a car accident in 1997 sent the world into a mass state of mourning.

Dire Straits

Named after their own financial situation when starting up, this British rock band led by Mark Knopfler went on to achieve international success. Their album *Brothers in Arms* was the biggest selling album of 1985 and became the first album to sell a million copies in CD format. Dire Straits had emerged on the back of the post-punk era of the late 70s but their roots really lay in bluesy pub rock. By the mid 80s their sound was more mature and refined and was seen by traditional rock fans as a welcome alternative to the high-energy, synthetic pop songs of the era.

Dirty Dancing

This coming of age romance from 1987 catapulted Patrick Swayze into superstardom and remains one of the best-loved movies of the era. Shot on a low budget of just £2.5million the story of Frances 'Baby' Houseman, a middle-class girl who falls in love with bad boy dance instructor Johnny Castle, has since grossed more than £150m and became the first film to sell a million copies on video. Set in an upmarket, predominantly Jewish American holiday camp in the Catskills, the script explored class barriers, back-street abortions and first love. Johnny helps Baby to shake off her middle-class reserve whilst teaching her to dance, and she teaches him that it is OK to stand up for yourself no matter what social class you belong to. The soundtrack featured the monster hit '(I've Had) The Time of My Life' which won an Oscar for Best Original Song while Swayze scored a number one hit with 'She's Like the Wind.' The lines 'Nobody puts Baby in the corner' and 'I carried a watermelon!' became iconic 80s catchphrases.

Disasters

Amongst the fun and frivolity of the 80s there were also some notable tragedies. Violence at football matches was a horrible reality during the 80s with English fans seen as particular offenders. On 29 May 1985 at Belgium's ageing Heysel Stadium 39 people died and hundreds were

PATRICK SWAYZE AND JENNIFER GREY IN *DIRTY DANCING.*

injured when a retaining wall collapsed under the weight of a contingent of Liverpool fans stampeding towards Juventus supporters. As a result all English clubs were banned from playing European football for five years, and Liverpool were banned for six years.

Also in 1985, a fire broke out in the Valley Parade football stadium in Bradford, during a match on 11 May between Bradford City and Lincoln City. Within four minutes of the fire starting, the whole stand was engulfed in flames. 56 people died and nearly 300 more were injured. The inquiry into the fire led to new legislation to improve safety at the UK's football grounds.

On April 26, 1986 a nuclear reactor at the Chernobyl nuclear plant in the USSR exploded. The resulting fire sent radioactive smoke into the atmosphere covering a vast geographical area with 400 times more fallout released than the atomic bombing of Hiroshima. It remains the worst nuclear accident in history.

1987 would see the tragic deaths of 193 passengers and crew when the Herald of Free Enterprise, a British passenger ferry capsized just outside the Belgium port of Zeebrugge. Many of the passengers were families who had taken advantage of promotions offering cheap travel to the continent.

The peace and tranquility of Hungerford, a market town 30 miles west of London, was shattered forever when resident Michael Ryan shot and killed 16 people on August 19, 1987. Armed with several weapons, including an AK–47, he shot his victims at random – including his own mother – before fatally shooting himself.

In the worst sporting disaster the UK has ever suffered, 96 Liverpool fans were crushed to death at Hillsborough Stadium on 15 April 1989. Hundreds more were injured on the steel-fenced terraces of Sheffield Wednesday's stadium, which was hosting that year's FA Cup semi-final. The inquiry into the disaster, led by Lord Chief Justice Taylor, established that main cause was a failure of police crowd control.

Dollar

Today, David Van Day might be mainly known as the 'snake in the grass' from *I'm A Celebrity: Get Me Out of Here*, but back in the 80s he made up half of the saccharine pop duo Dollar. Sharing the limelight with his real–life girlfriend Thereza Bazar caused friction and the couple had a famously tempestuous relationship on and off stage. Teaming up with legendary pop producer Trevor Horn in 1980 proved very lucrative and the couple sold 10 million records with hits including 'Give Me Back My Heart' and 'Mirror Mirror'. But on a promotional tour in Japan in 1983, relations between the couple hit a new low and Van Day walked out.

Donovan, Jason

This wholesome-looking hunk from Down Under stole a million British hearts playing Kylie Minogue's love interest in the Aussie soap *Neighbours*. The pair cashed in on their on-screen romance by releasing 'Especially For You', a soppy duet that was to hit the number one spot in 1988. Never achieving the same level of success as Kylie,

JASON DONOVAN AND KYLIE MINOGUE SHARE A KISS ON *NEIGHBOURS*.

Jason nevertheless released a number one solo album *Ten Good Reasons* in 1989. Donovan has admitted that by the early 90s he had developed a drug problem, and he collapsed from a cocaine-induced seizure at Kate Moss's 21st birthday party in Hollywood. He has been free of drugs since the birth of his first child in 2000, however, and came third in the TV reality show *I'm A Celebrity: Get Me Out of Here* in 2006.

Do the Right Thing

Spike Lee wrote and directed this observation of racial attitudes in 1989. He examines the racism that he claims is always bubbling beneath the surface in American society. The action begins on a blistering hot New York day and centres on Sal's Famous Pizzeria, which has existed for a quarter of a century in the neighbourhood and is run by Sal (Danny Aiello) and his two sons. A black activist known as Buggin' Out demands that Sal's is boycotted when he notices that the pizzeria's wall of fame is lacking in black personalities. Sal states that as an Italian, he has the right to celebrate his heritage by only featuring Italians on the wall. At first no one takes any notice of the dispute, but gradually people take sides and the movie ends in racial violence. Have attitudes and beliefs changed in the past twenty years since the movie was shot? Has progress been made? It's hard to say with any certainty, but back then Barack Obama would never have been elected

President of the United States so some things have definitely changed for the better.

Dukes of Hazzard

Imported from America and one of the most popular 1980s series on British television, Gy Waldron's creation was based on an earlier film he'd made called Moonrunners. More like a comic strip for teenagers than an adult comedy series, the show was designed to pinpoint the fantasies of the average teenager. The series followed the adventures of Bo and Luke Duke in the fictional country of Hazzard in rural Georgia as they roared around in their super charged automobile, The General Lee. Their adversaries were the stupid sheriff, Rosco P. Coltrane, and the corrupt County Commissioner, Boss Hogg. As a punishment for making moonshine the boys are forbidden to carry firearms so they make up for it by arming themselves with bows and arrow tipped with dynamite. The show was also liberally sprinkled with scantily dressed and improbably beautiful girls.

Duran Duran

With girly haircuts, expertly applied eyeliner and elegant designer clothes it's no wonder this group earned themselves the nickname 'the prettiest boys in rock'. But behind the flamboyant outer images these guys were a musical force to be reckoned with and stand out as one of the most successful bands of the decade, selling more than 100 million records. Fronted by Simon Le Bon, it was the video for their third single 'Girls on Film' that really got them noticed. Made by the innovative directing duo Godley & Creme, it featured semi-naked women pillow fighting and mud wrestling and was banned by the BBC.

With the release of their second album *Rio*, Duran Duran began to achieve worldwide recognition in 1982. It scored four UK Top Twenty singles with 'My Own Way', 'Hungry Like the Wolf', 'Save a Prayer' and the title song 'Rio' and a headlining tour of Australia, Japan, and the U.S followed. Princess Diana declared they were her favourite band and the press began to refer to them as 'The Fab Five' likening their success to Beatlemania. Four more albums followed and in 1989 they released *Decade*, essentially a greatest hits album, which charted their phenomenal success throughout the 80s.

Dynasty

Over-the-top storylines, catfights, impossibly large shoulder pads and even an alien abduction helped make *Dynasty* one of the decade's most talked about US soaps. Starring John Forsythe and Linda Evans as newlyweds Blake and Krystle Carrington, the show was written as a rival to Dallas and centred on the trials and tribulations of the super-wealthy Carrington and Colby families. More

DYNASTY

daring and showy than *Dallas*, *Dynasty* personified the glamour and glitz of the 80s and relaunched Joan Collins's career. After appearing in the 70s soft-porn movies *The Stud* and *The Bitch*, Collins's star was definitely on the wane. Looking for a way to boost the ratings of the second season, producers hired Collins as Alexis, the scheming, grasping and super bitchy ex-wife of the Blake Carrington. Collins and *Dynasty* were made for each other and soon it was Number one in the ratings. Further proof of its popularity came when former President Gerald Ford and Secretary of State Henry Kissinger appeared as themselves playing friends of Alexis and producers cashed in with commercial spin-offs like the haute couture Dynasty Collection and monogrammed towels and sheets.

EastEnders

The nation's love affair with Albert Square began on a chilly February evening in 1985, when several male characters burst into the bedsit of a missing pensioner to find that he had been murdered. The show, created by producer Julia Smith and script editor Tony Holland, was first screened in twice-weekly half-hour slots with a an hour-long repeat omnibus on Sunday afternoon. Centred on the inhabitants of Albert Square in the fictional London borough of Walford, *EastEnders* was an immediate smash hit, attracting initial viewing figures of 17 million. Less than two years later, the 1986 Christmas episode, in which pub landlord Den Watts served his wife Angie with divorce papers, drew an audience of more than 30 million. This made it the most watched soap episode in

UK history and *EastEnders* the highest rated soap opera of the decade.

Gritty storylines included murder, drug addiction and prostitution. When 16-year-old Michelle Fowler (Susan Tully) became pregnant the nation waited with bated breath, until it was revealed that her baby's father was Den Watts, the father of her best friend Sharon (Letitia Dean). That little indiscretion earned him the nickname Dirty Den. The story made the front page of almost every UK newspaper, a previously unheard of phenomenon and catapulted actor Leslie Grantham to not only national heartthrob but near superstar status.

Best Loved EastEnders Characters

The Fowlers and the Beales
Matriarch Lou Beale was mother to twins Pauline Fowler and Peter Beale. She lived with daughter Pauline, hen-pecked son-in-law Arthur and grandchildren Michelle and Mark.

Son Peter lived in a nearby tower block with his second wife Kathy and his son Ian, the apple of Lou's eye.

The Watts
Adulterer Den Watts lived with wayward alcoholic wife Angie and sluttish, attention seeking daughter, Sharon. As landlords of local pub, the Queen Victoria, many of the soap's high jinks and dramas occurred in and around the Watts' place of work and home.

Ethel and Dot

Childhood friends with Lou Beale, Ethel and Dot were the resident old dears of Albert Square. Dot's morose hypochondria made her the perfect contrast to Ethel's childlike, joyful nature.

Nick Cotton

'Nasty' Nick Cotton, the dastardly son of poor old Dot, was a wrong'un and an almost operatic villain. We loved to hate him and gasped at the terrible tricks he pulled whenever he got the chance.

The pets

Roly the standard poodle lived with the Watts family above the Queen Vic. The darling of the square, he led owners Den and Angie a merry dance whilst he cavorted with Ethel's greedy Pug, Little Willie Skinner.

Easton, Sheena

After appearing in an episode of a TV programme *The Big Time*, which showed her attempts to secure a record deal, the diminutive Scottish singer eventually achieved worldwide fame after signing a contract with EMI Records and recording singles such as 'Modern Girl', '9 to 5' and the Bond movie theme 'For Your Eyes Only'. Her popularity increased more in the USA and Japan and she eventually left the UK for America, where she managed to shrug off her rather wholesome image and have her Prince-penned single, 'Sugar Walls', denounced as 'filthy' by the Vice-President's wife, Tipper Gore.

Echo & the Bunnymen

Known for their distinctive, alternative sound with a drum machine beat, Echo and the Bunnymen were a post-punk band from Liverpool consisting of singer Ian McCulloch, guitarist Will Sergeant, bass player Les Pattinson and drummer Pete de Freitas. Achieving their first success on the alternative music scene they became a mainstream hit in 1982 with the singles 'The Back Of Love' and 'The Cutter' which reached No.19 and No. 8 respectively in the UK charts. Their LP *Porcupine* reached number two in the album charts. Their success continued with 1984's cult album *Ocean Rain*.

They split in 1988 after McCulloch left the band and in 1989 27-year-old Pete de Freitas was tragically killed in a motorcycle accident.

Ecstasy

With the emergence of the Acid House dance craze, the UK was suddenly flooded with previously unheard-of psychoactive drug MDMA, going by the street name ecstasy. Said to induce a feeling of euphoria and empathy, the amphetamine-based drug allowed users to dance all night after entering a trance-like state and was popular amongst clubbers. Gradually, the dangerous side affects became known as many users danced themselves to exhaustion or dehydration, and some died. The long-term mental health problems associated with the use of MDMA then became apparent.

Enfield, Harry

Harry Enfield's first television success came with his appearances on Channel 4's *Friday Night Live*, where he introduced comedy characters including Stavros, an amiable Greek kebab shop owner, and loutish Tory voting, boastful Loadsamoney. Massively successful, the nation's youth adopted Enfield's characters' catch phrases, often emulating him by shouting, 'Loadsamoney', while waving fistfuls of £20 notes!

Erasure

This high-energy, synth-pop duo was formed in 1985 by singer Andy Bell and keyboard player Vince Clarke, who had been a founding member of Depeche Mode and Yazoo.

After initial, modest success, they entered the 80s hall of fame with the release in 1988 of their third album, *The Innocents*, a double-platinum UK hit that gave us the singles 'Chains of Love' and 'A Little Respect'. Massive dance club hits, the two songs reached the UK Top Ten and the Top 20 in the US Charts.

E.T., The Extra-Terrestrial

Steven Spielberg's 1982 science fiction movie has also been called 'Spielberg's love story', and some interpret it as an allegory of the story of Christ. Whatever the truth, there can be no denying that the most successful movie of all time was utterly magical and continues to charm generation after generation. The poignant story of lonely, fatherless Elliott's tender friendship with elderly, stranded alien E.T. gave us actress Drew Barrymore's first movie appearance as Elliott's five year old sister Gertie and was responsible for a million croaky voice renditions of the catchphrase, 'E.T., phone home.'

Eurythmics

The wildly successful pop-rock duo of singer, Annie Lennox and multi-instrumental songwriter Dave Stewart had their first success with the worldwide hit 'Sweet Dreams (Are Made of This)'. The video featured an androgynous Annie Lennox with close-cropped red hair, dressed in a man's suit and wielding a cane. This gender-bending image would return through many of Eurythmics' subsequent videos. Annie Lennox subsequently had a successful solo career, for which she adopted a more feminine image – although she has never been mainstream in her look.

E.T., THE EXTRA-TERRESTRIAL

Face, The

Anybody who was anybody was desperate to appear in this fashion and style bible. Launched in 1980 by Nick Logan, previous editor of *NME* and the creator of *Smash Hits*, *The Face* started life as a rock magazine but encompassed youth culture, fashion, art, attitudes and growing trends. 80s heartthrob Jason Donovan successfully sued the magazine for libel when it suggested he was gay and the damages and court costs nearly forced the magazine to close. It eventually did close in 2004 but many of its front covers are considered collectors items and are perfect examples of 80s nostalgia.

Falklands War

The seemingly endless fun and frivolity of the early 1980s was shattered when Britain was drawn into a bloody conflict after an Argentine naval force invaded the Falkland Islands on April 2 1982. Argentine President Leopoldo Galtieri believed that the British Government would not go to war over a small cluster of islands where sheep far outnumbered inhabitants. He was wrong. The government immediately announced it would fight to reclaim the islands, launching a naval task force, and within three days ships and troops were on their way to the Falklands. In scenes reminiscent of the Second World War, TV cameras captured tearful wives and families waving their men off to war from UK military bases.

Air raids were mounted against the Islands' capital, Port Stanley, and the British nuclear submarine HMS Conqueror sank Argentine ship General Belgrano, killing 368 men. The Argentines retaliated by destroying HMS Sheffield and sinking HMS Ardent, Antelope and Coventry. British Forces advanced on Port Stanley on 12th June and two days later the Argentines surrendered. The conflict had lasted 74 days and resulted in the loss of 236 British soldiers and 655 from Argentina.

FAME

Following the 1980 movie and the subsequent TV spin-off, it seemed every kid in the country was suddenly stage struck and wearing legwarmers. With the iconic voiceover 'You want fame? Well, fame costs and right here's where you start paying ... with sweat!' ringing in their ears, *The Kids from Fame* captured the imagination and essence of the go-getting 80s. Based around the hopes and ambitions of a bunch of wannabe students at New York's High School for Performing Arts, *Fame* was the forerunner of recent hits such as *High School Musical* and *Glee*. The original movie was gritty and dark containing abortion, suicide and child abuse storylines but the TV show presented a much more wholesome, frothy and sanitised version of life in the Big Apple. Songs performed in the show including 'Fame', 'Starmaker' and 'Hi-Fidelity' hit the British Charts and the ensemble embarked on a sell-out UK tour.

Fashion

New Romantics

The first big fashion statement of the 80s began in the London club Blitz, where members sought a new style to contrast with the slovenliness and vulgarity of punk. The look they devised soon saw them described as the New Romantics. Imaginatively plundering fashions from the more recent past as well as historical costumes, they blended it all with futuristic make-up to achieve the startling effects they desired, from the ghostly appearance

GEORGE CLOONEY EPITOMISES THE 80S FASHION IN HIS CHECKED
JUMPER IN 1987.

of a World War II pilot to the berets, striped tops, tight skirts and black stockings worn by the Apache dancers of Paris's underworld. The New Romantic look set no boundaries of style; devotees could as easily appear as a fairy tale princess with garish make-up or as an androgynous Harlequin. Inspired by the movement, designers Vivienne Westwood and Malcolm McLaren devised a pirate look, especially for the pop group Adam and the Ants that featured full-sleeved ruffled shirts, Hussar-style jackets in theatrical velvet, and long suede boots. Spandau Ballet were also pioneers of the look, and it was soon taken up in the High Street as New Romanticism moved into the mainstream of fashion.

Dancewear

After the popularity of *Flashdance* and *The Kids from Fame*, dancewear began to be worn on the streets: leotards, leggings and of course, legwarmers, which were often worn over jeans in a variety of lurid colours. Part of the look was an oversized sweatshirt revealing one bare shoulder – and that was just the boys!

Fitness wear

With Jane Fonda's best-selling workout book and the birth of aerobics, cat suits made in shiny Lycra were adopted as a fashion to be worn outside the gym. A neon-coloured sweatband often completed the look.

Ra-Ra Skirts

Inspired by American cheerleaders and the success of Tony Basil's song 'Mickey', ra-ra skirts proved to be a big hit with teenage girls. In a variety of materials and colours, some came with matching sweatshirts. Both day and night wear, they were seen in the winter with tights and flat-heeled pixie boots, in the summer with bare legs and pumps and, tragically, sometimes with white ankle socks and stilettos.

Pixie Boots

Suede ankle boots with a cuff.

The Shell Suit

A hideous sport suit of nylon trousers with matching zipped jacket, they were often worn in lurid and contrasting colour combinations, purple and yellow being a popular choice.

The 'Miami Vice' Look

Based on the clothes worn by actors in the hit TV show it comprised unstructured blazers or suits (often designed by Armani) worn with pastel T-shirts and Gucci loafers without socks.

Power Dressing

Hair was big and so were shoulders! Heavily influenced by soaps such as *Dynasty* and *Dallas*, the power dresser was a product of the 80s economy boom. She had money and she dressed to show it off wearing boxy jackets, always with shoulder pads, the highest heels and chunky jewellery. At night she dressed the same, but with the addition of sequins and barely there, sheer black tights.

Anything Worn By Princess Diana

From her wedding dress on, everything she was photographed in was immediately copied and available on the high street within days.

Underwear as Outerwear

Bras, bustiers, corsets and camisoles worn, sometimes with a leather jacket, often with a large crucifix necklace, tons of bangles and huge, hoop earrings, a lace rag in the hair, net skirts over leggings and fingerless gloves. Thank you Madonna!

Patterned Tights

Lacy, spotty, stripy, they could be delicate or garish. Sometimes they were embellished at with diamante.

Coloured Tights

In sheer, woollen and opaque coloured tights were often coordinated with matching shoes.

Hats

From Princess Di-style veiled pillboxes to straw boaters and berets, hats were popular throughout the decade.

Denim

Stonewashed jeans (ready faded) were massively popular in the 1980s as were ripped jeans. The really daring would cut down their jeans to shorts, adding a rip on the bum!

Boxer Shorts and Designer Pants

In 1985 it was out with the Y-fronts when a seriously sexy Nick Kamen stripped down to his boxer shorts in a Levi's commercial. Sales of the undergarment went sky high as young men and their girlfriends stampeded to buy them. Calvin Klein pants, for both men and women, were popular after Michael J Fox wore them in *Back To The Future*.

Hair

Worn big and backcombed or short and spiky, hairstyles in the 80s could be bafflingly eccentric as pop group A Flock Of Seagulls proved. The absurd mullet trend had several variations all based on the same short at the sides long at the back style. It was an era of perms that frazzled long hair in an attempt at Pre-Raphaelite loveliness. If it wasn't permed it was backcombed and sprayed with so much hairspray it stayed in place for days. Less time consuming but no better for condition was crimping: an effect that supposedly gave hair body and waves but in reality made it resemble corrugated iron! As the years passed, flattops were the popular choice for young men and sleek bobs for girls (think Robert Palmer's 'Addicted to Love' video).

Specially made mascara added coloured streaks to hair and the most popular choice for teenagers when home dying was aubergine/plum.

Ray-Ban Wayfarer Sunglasses

As worn by Tom Cruise in *Risky Business*, yearly sales of the black sunglasses rose from barely 18,000 in 1981 to a massive 360,000 just two years later. They were the 1980s shades of choice.

Make-Up

The New Romantic style fantasy make-up seen in clubs eventually gave way to a dark eyed, red-lipped vampish look. Lashings of blue mascara and pink frosted lipstick as well as an abundance of silvers and golds decorated faces until and a new craze for a natural, sun kissed look became popular with the release of bronzing powders.

Fast Times at Ridgemont High

We're used to investigative reporters going undercover to expose corruption and vice, but *Rolling Stone* reporter Cameron Crowe had another target in mind when he went back to a Californian high school to

SEAN PENN IN *FAST TIMES
AT RIDGEMONT HIGH*

record the antics of the student body. Instead of a coruscating drama he exposed the bitter/sweet comedy of the young, with huge success. He turned his own book into a screenplay and the subsequent movie became a smash hit of 1982. Several stars of the future took minor roles: Sean Penn, Nicholas Cage, Eric Stoltz, Forrest Whitaker, Anthony Edwards, Judge Reinhold, and Jennifer Jason Leigh. The story line is uncomplicated; it simply follows the ups and downs of the kids for a year. Sean Penn earns an extra mention with his cameo role as the permanently stoned surfer drifting through life.

Fatal Attraction

Writer James Dearden and director Adrian Lyne prepared two endings for this 1987 thriller. Although they finally went with the softer option the movie still, as Tom Hanks's character in *Sleepless in Seattle* claims, '…scared every man in America.'

The plot is simple but the pace of action grasps like a vice. A happily married man, played by Michael Douglas, is away from home on a business trip and meets an attractive, intelligent woman, played by Glenn Close, who offers him a one night stand with absolutely no strings attached. He falls for her seduction, only to later discover that she is mentally deranged and has become obsessed by her 'victim'. Pursuing him to his home she begins a frightening campaign of terror, including the memorable murder of the family's pet rabbit, which gave rise to the popular phrase 'bunny boiler' to describe an obsessive ex. Finally, the stalker is destroyed, but the alternative ending had her committing suicide and framing the errant husband for murder.

Ferris Bueller's Day Off

Comedies about teenage rebellion were big business in the 80s but Ferris was undoubtedly this genre's favourite hero. Played with effortless charm by Matthew Broderick, Ferris is a truanting school kid with a difference. Whilst many teen movies of the time dealt with raging hormones, unrequited love and difficult family relationships, this movie is about a kid who simply wants to enjoy the cultural delights of Chicago. Feigning illness and using ingenious methods to avoid his suspicious headmaster, Ferris, his girlfriend Sloane and best friend Cameron hit the city in a vintage Ferrari 'borrowed' from Cameron's dad. Along the way they dine in Chicago's finest restaurant, take in a baseball game, visit the Art Institute and hijack a carnival float resulting in Ferris hilariously lip-synching to Wayne Newton's 'Danke Schoen' to an adoring crowd. Made on a very low budget by comedy genius John Hughes, it was one of the top grossing movies of the year and beautifully captures the joy of adolescence, the charms of Chicago and sums up the exciting, new prospects that were facing 80s teenagers.

Filofax

First sold in 1921, a British company manufactured Filofax and the name was abbreviated from 'File of Facts'. Traditionally bound in leather, this spiral bound personal organiser is divided into sections for the efficient storage of retrievable information. Its popularity grew enormously in the early 80s when it was closely identified as one of the essential pieces of equipment that denoted the owner was a yuppie.

First Blood

Directed by Ted Kotcheff, this was the first, and by far the best, of the Rambo movies. Made in 1982, when memories of the Vietnam War were still haunting America, the story concerns an army veteran, John J. Rambo, who is harassed by the sheriff of a small Oregon town when he is attempting to contact an old friend. The sheriff, played by Brian Dennehy, orders him to move on, but Rambo digs in his heels. The sheriff arrests him and while he's in jail one of the deputies mistreats him. Rambo, a former Green Beret, snaps and breaks out of jail to flee into the rugged countryside. The sheriff and his men pursue him but they are no match for Rambo. Finally they have to call

Madonna was the
defining 80s music icon.
Here she is in 1984.

Just some of the many changing looks of Madonna in the 1980s.

More 80s Music Icons:
Above left: Janet Jackson in 1981.

Above right: Chrissie Hynde of The Pretenders.

Below: Freddie Mercury and Queen.

Formed in 1984, New Kids on the Block had their first No. 1 Billboard Hot 100 single with 'I'll Be Loving You (Forever)' right at the end of the decade.

Eurythmics was made up of Scottish frontwoman Annie Lennox (pictured) and English musician Dave Stewart. Their most famous single, 'Sweet Dreams (Are Made of This)' was released in 1983.

Some of the best movies in the 80s were great love stories.
Above: Patrick Swayze and Jennifer Grey in the famous 'lift' scene
of *Dirty Dancing* (1987).

Below: Tom Cruise and Kelly McGillis were another popular 80s movie
couple in *Top Gun* (1986).

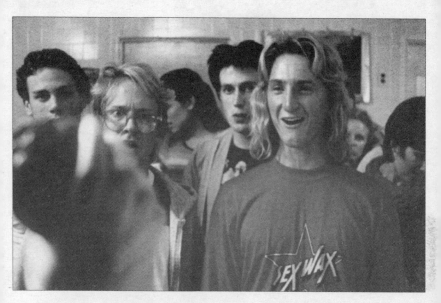

80s Movie Icons:

Above: Scott Thomas as Arnold and Sean Penn as Jeff Spicoli in the high school movie *Fast Times at Ridgemont High* (1982).

Below: Matthew Broderick in *Ferris Bueller's Day Off* (1986), with director John Hughes.

80s Movie Icons:
Above: Meryl Streep and Cher starred in the movie *Silkwood* (1983).

Below: Wil Wheaton (as Gordie), River Phoenix (as Chris), Corey Feldman (as Teddy) and Jerry O'Connell (as Vern) in the classic 80s coming-of-age flick *Stand By Me* (1986).

in the National Guard, who also prove to be ineffectual against the killing machine they have unleashed. Eventually the conflict between the sheriff and Rambo leads to a final confrontation, when Rambo all but destroys the town.

Five Star

Seen as Britain's answer to the Jackson Five, this bunch of smiley siblings from Romford in Essex seemed to have the world at their feet in 1985. Famous for heavily choreographed dance routines and matching avant-garde outfits the group was put together by their father Buster Pearson and achieved a string of Top 40 hits. As their popularity waned they ditched their formerly clean-cut image in favour of an edgier look and added a harder dance sound to their music but sadly it couldn't keep the wolves from the door and under a media spotlight the band were declared bankrupt.

Flashdance

This ultimate 'American Dream' movie saw exquisitely pretty Alex, a welder by day and strip club dancer by night, trying to make it in classical ballet. After flunking her original audition for a prestigious dance academy, Alex, played by Jennifer Beal, almost gives up on her dreams. But after falling in love with her hunky boss and listening to

JENNIFER BEAL IN *FLASHDANCE*.

some inspirational advice from her dying dance mentor, Alex decides to do things her way and stuns the judges at a later audition with her own style of contemporary and outlandish dance moves. The previous success of *Fame*, a prize soundtrack and visually stunning and creatively choreographed dance sequences, guaranteed this movie a big box office return.

Footloose

Kevin Bacon may be known today as the star of gritty dramas and thrillers but back in 1984 he was tripping the light fantastic as a Ren 'Footloose' McCormack, a swivel-hipped, music obsessed teenager who moves to a small country town where rock music and dancing is banned. Footloose tries to get the town's evil minister to relax the rules and wins his daughter's heart along the way. The film was loosely based on the real life rural town of Elmore City in Oklahoma where dancing was banned for 100 years. In 1980, the ban was lifted and that year's graduating students made history by being the first students allowed to dance at the High School Prom.

Fox, Samantha

Back in the 80s the words 'Page Three' meant boobs, and boobs meant Sam Fox. The diminutive glamour model flaunted her impressive bust in countless newspapers and

KEVIN BACON IN *FOOTLOOSE.*

personal appearances and her chirpy cockney, down-to-earth personality helped make her the most popular and successful glamour model of all time. She retired from topless modelling in 1986 aged just 20 and broke into the music business, making three albums and scoring three top ten hits.

Frankie Goes to Hollywood

Backed by an ingenious marketing campaign, this band from Liverpool, fronted by Holly Johnson, burst onto the dance-pop music scene in 1984 creating controversy from day one. Famously banned by the BBC, their first single 'Relax', with its explicit video and lyrics pertaining to gay sex, charted at Number one for five consecutive weeks. The band's promotional director had designed T-shirts bearing the logos 'Relax' and 'Frankie Says...' to coincide with the single's release and they immediately swept the country. Actively courting notoriety, their follow up single 'Two Tribes', with its anti-conflict message and blaring air raid sirens, again featured a risqué video depicting Cold War leaders Ronald Reagan and Konstantin Chernenko wrestling in a makeshift ring with onlookers aggressively egging them on. Again FGTH had a massive hit on their hands and when they released 'The Power of Love', a slower-paced romantic ballad, they scored a hat trick of number ones.

French and Saunders

A new kind of entertainment emerged in the early 80s which became known as Alternative Comedy, and this young double act was at the forefront. Dawn French and Jennifer Saunders formed a professional partnership after meeting at drama school and began performing at the infamous London club The Comedy Store, where many underground acts were honing their material. Their pairing was to be one of the most successful in UK history and their BBC sketch show was given unprecedented budgets to create elaborate, hilarious parodies of mainstream culture and celebrities including Madonna, Bananarama and Abba. The *French and Saunders* sketch show ran for six years and although both women went on to enjoy huge success individually, they have frequently reunited for one-off specials.

Friday the 13th

1980 gave us the first teenage slasher movie, a genre that was to plod on for twelve ghastly sequels over the ensuing twenty-five years. The action takes place at Camp Crystal Lake, where a new teenage intake has come to holiday at the location of two gruesome murders, and there are more on the way. Despite the menace the boys and girls gradually give rein to their sexual desires, only to pay an awful price for their inability to suppress their instincts. For fans of slasher

JASON VORHEES FROM THE *FRIDAY THE 13TH* MOVIES.

movies this is a classic: many others will wonder at the crassness of it all.

Fry, Stephen

Stephen John Fry, who was born on 24 August 1957, is one of those astonishingly talented people who seem able to excel in any sphere that interests them. Born in Hampstead, he moved to Norfolk as a child, a part of the country which he loves and to where he constantly returns. Fry's mother's parents were Jewish and came from a place which is now part of Slovakia. Her aunt and cousins died in Auschwitz.

Although a brilliantly clever boy, Fry was expelled from Uppingham public school, and after attending Norfolk College of Arts and Technology for a time, he made off with a credit card taken from a family friend. As a consequence he spent three months on remand in Pucklechurch Prison.

Following his release he knuckled down and attended the City College Norwich, where he gained a scholarship to Queen's College, Cambridge.

Joining Cambridge Footlights, he met his future collaborator and comedy partner Hugh Laurie. They went on to write *The Cellar Tapes* for Footlights in 1980/81. It proved to be a big hit at the Edinburgh Festival and won the Perrier Comedy Award. In the 1980s Stephen Fry's career really took off. He was a central member of the cast of *Blackadder* and the comedy sketch series *A Bit of Fry and Laurie* was a big success when it first aired in 1989. Such a workload would be enough for most people, but Stephen Fry also wrote plays and books and appeared in television commercials and in the theatre, as well as providing endless voiceovers. He was much in demand on radio, as well as appearing in movies.

Gabriel, Peter

A founding member of avant-garde rock group Genesis, Gabriel turned solo and achieved his greatest popularity in the mid 80s. His 1986 album *So* produced several transatlantic hits including 'Big Time, Don't Give Up' in which he sang a duet with Kate Bush, and 'Sledgehammer', the winner of nine MTV Video Music Awards and ranked number four in the MTV '100 Greatest Music Videos Ever Made'. Featuring pixilation and frame-by-frame animation, Gabriel had to lie under a sheet of glass for 16 hours during filming!

Gang of Four

To huge media attention, in 1981 four major Labour Party figures, David Owen, Roy Jenkins, Bill Rodgers and Shirley Williams, broke away from the Labour Party, claiming they were alarmed by the swing to the left led by Michael Foot. Vowing they would unite the country and bring a new direction to British politics the four announced the formation of the Social Democratic Party. There was an initial surge of support from disenchanted voters, but they soon settled down to being just another minority party without any parliamentary power. The SDP was dissolved in 1988 when, after an alliance of several years, they finally merged with the Liberal Party to form the Liberal Democrats.

Ghostbusters

This Dan Aykroyd/Harold Ramis-penned comedy was the story of four inept parapsychologists who set themselves up as 'expert ghost exterminators' promising to rid haunted buildings of unwanted spirit guests. When Manhattan suffers a major spate of terrifying hauntings, the Ghostbusters find themselves inundated with work and are clueless as to how they should carry it out. The theme song of the same name by Ray Parker Jr was number one in the US for three weeks and number two in the UK. The movie spawned a 1989 sequel, two

BILL MURRAY IN *GHOSTBUSTERS*.

animated television series, two novelisations, several comic books and numerous toys.

Gibson, Debbie

Signed to Atlantic records at the tender age of 16, Debbie Gibson was a prototype Britney Spears – everybody's kid sister's favourite pop idol. Her debut album *Out of the Blue* was entirely her own composition and she performed some rather arduous dances with her backing singers whilst performing live. Her career as a pop star never made it past the end of the 80s though she did find later success acting in musical theatre on Broadway and London's West End.

Grange Hill

Phil Redmond approached all fifteen ITV companies with the idea for a gritty documentary style children's series set in a comprehensive school, and each one turned him down. Luckily the BBC was looking for a school series and so the legend was born. He originally wanted to call the show *Grange Park* and set it in Liverpool, but there were too many schools with the same name and it proved impractical for the BBC to produce the show outside London. The series proved to be so controversial in the 80s that many adults complained to the BBC and several celebrities banned their children from watching, including the newscaster Anna Ford. But *Grange Hill* went from strength to strength and set new standards for children's drama. It became so iconic that Ben Elton paid it the ultimate compliment of parodying the show in an episode of *The Young Ones*.

Great Storm, The

On October 15 1987, Michael Fish, the BBC weatherman, made the most quoted (and misquoted) weather prediction of all time. He said: 'Earlier on today, apparently, a woman rang the BBC and said she heard there was a hurricane on the way ... well, if you're watching, don't worry, there isn't!' He went on to warn that there would be strong winds and told viewers to 'batten down the hatches', but this was forgotten as within a few hours southern England was battered by – although not a hurricane – the worst storm to hit the country in the 20th century. The devastation was appalling. With winds gusting up to 110 miles an hour, 17 people lost their lives. The ground had absorbed an unusually large amount of rain, and the mild autumn had seen trees retain their leaves so that they caught the wind and were blown out of the ground. The town of Sevenoaks lost the oak trees that gave it its name, Kew Gardens was denuded of a third of its rare and valuable trees, and in some areas whole swathes of the countryside were altered beyond recognition.

Greenham Common Women's Peace Camp

In September 1981 in the genteel English county of Berkshire 36 members of a Welsh activist group called 'Women for Life on Earth' arrived at the RAF base at

Greenham Common, to protest at the government's decision to allow 96 NATO Cruise Missiles to be based there. They had marched from Cardiff to deliver a letter to the base commander stating their fear for their children and for the world. With repeated requests for a debate ignored they set up a peace camp in close proximity to the fence that surrounded the compound.

The Welsh walkers also gained media attention by chaining themselves to the base fence and as word spread more, more protestors arrived to lend their support.

Using the tactical measure of non-violent protest, by the latter half of 1982 the numbers had grown by 30,000. As time passed the camp divided into nine segments named after the colours of the rainbow. In April 1983, about 70,000 people made a 14 mile human chain from Greenham to RAF Aldermaston and the ordnance factory at Burghfield.

The women often suffered violence, but refused to give up. Whether it was threading paper doves of peace and baby bonnets through the fences, lying down in front of lorries or bolt-cutting the camp fence to exercise their right to walk on common land, they persisted in their protest. As the first cruise missiles arrived 50,000 women encircled the camp. Many were arrested, fined heavily and even imprisoned.

The camp remained at the common for 19 years, a witness to the arrival and eventual exit of the last weapons, finally closing in 2000. A business park now stands where the airbase once was and a memorial is all that remains of the Peace Camp. The rest of the land has returned to common ground, meaning anybody can come and go, to enjoy the countryside at their leisure.

Gregory's Girl

Gentle and hilarious, this coming of age romance was written and directed by John Forsyth. Set in Scotland it starred John Gordon Sinclair as gawky and amiable teenager Gregory. Not at all cool and quite shy, Gregory is mortified when his place on the school football team is given to gorgeous Dorothy (Dee Dawson), the prettiest girl in school. Whilst plotting to win Dorothy's heart he meets Susan (Clare Grogan) who the audience can see is clearly made for him. *Gregory's Girl* is poignant, innocent and very funny, like many people's memories of growing up in the 80s.

Gremlins

Director Joe Dante brought this anti-Christmas story to the screen in 1984 featuring a strange but lovable pet bought in Chinatown and taken home to a typical American suburb, where it transforms itself into a plague of mischievously destructive creatures that bring havoc in their wake. Originally there was a scene planned where the gremlins would invade a McDonald's and eat all the customers, leaving the hamburgers intact. But that was considered to strong and the makers decided to soften the image slightly. Originally, the term 'gremlin' was much used during World War II to describe the irritating glitches that interfered with production in war plants.

Haircut 100

Just as the New Wave movement was peaking this cheerful, fresh-faced group appeared fronted by boyish heart-throb Nick Heyward. Their songs, including 'Love Plus One' and 'Fantastic Day', contained joyful melodies and chirpy lyrics and were an antidote to the more serious and politically minded bands of the early 80s.

Happy Mondays

Fronted by the hugely talented but troubled songwriter Shaun Ryder, this band invented an alternative dance/rock sound that was heartily embraced by the Rave Scene of the late 80s. Blending Indie guitar riffs with Northern

Soul and Funk rhythms they soon entered the mainstream music charts. Songs such as '24 Hour Party People' set them apart from other rock bands of the era. Discovered by musical impresario Tony Wilson during a 'battle of the bands' contest held at his infamous Manchester nightspot The Hacienda, they were later to sign to his Factory Records Label – Wilson signing the contract in his own blood to prove his faith in them.

Hardcastle, Paul

It was n-n-n-n-nineteen eighty-five and this British composer and creative synthesiser specialist brought us our first taste of musical stuttering. Innovative at the time, the track called '19' referred to the average age of the soldiers killed in the Vietnam War. It consisted of a dance backtrack overlaid with samples of dialogue taken from a television documentary outlaying the post traumatic stress suffered by veterans. It topped the chart for five weeks and although he was never to achieve another number one, Hardcastle went on to forge a successful career in producing, remixing and composing television theme tunes.

Haysi Fantayzee

This heavily stylised New Wave pop group scored hits with quirky songs 'John Wayne is Big Leggy', 'Sister

Friction' and 'Shiny Shiny'. Fronted by white dreadlocked singers Kate Garner and Jeremiah Healy, it was their ragamuffin, thrift-shop fashion sense and not their music that set them apart. The act was also overshadowed by the appearance of Boy George whose fashion style was uncannily similar to theirs and during a 1983 interview Healy accused the Culture Club singer of stealing their look.

Heaven 17

After parting company with their first group The Human League in 1980, Craig Marsh and Martyn Ware set up the production company British Electric Foundation and recruited their friend Glenn Gregory as their vocalist. They named their new synth pop incarnation Heaven 17 after a fictional band from the Anthony Burgess novel *A Clockwork Orange*. Struggling at first to make an impact on the music charts their fortunes changed with the release of the single 'Temptation'. Owing much to the powerful, almost operatic vocals of Glenn Gregory and Carol Kenyon, 'Temptation' was to be their biggest hit charting at number two in the spring of 1983. Towards the end of that year, using the guise of British Electric Foundation, the band helped relaunch Tina Turner's career by producing and providing backing vocals on her comeback hit 'Let's Stay Together'.

Hit Factory, The

It was almost impossible to turn on a radio in the late 80s without hearing a Stock Aitken and Waterman track. Churning out chart toppers with staggering regularity, this trio, comprising Pete Waterman, Matt Aitken and Mike Stock, earned themselves the nickname 'The Hit Factory'. Their distinctive brand of catchy, bubblegum pop was criticised for being formulaic but Waterman defended their style, comparing their production-line output to that of Motown two decades earlier. 80s pop sensations Kylie Minogue, Rick Astley, Bananarama, Mel and Kim and Brother Beyond were just a few of the acts created by SAW. With more than 200 UK hit singles they go down in the 80s hall of fame as the most successful song writing and producing partnership of all time.

Hothouse Flowers

Originally called the Incomparable Benzini Brothers, this Irish group began performing by busking on the streets of Dublin. Formed by school friends Liam Ó Maonlaí and Fiachna Ó Braonáin, they combined traditional Irish folk, rock and gospel giving them a distinctive musical edge. Described in 1986 by Rolling Stone Magazine as 'the best unsigned band in Europe' they were soon noticed by U2 front man and rock legend Bono. After signing them to U2's Mother Records their first single 'Love Don't Work this Way' led to a deal with Polygram records where they made their first album *People* which was the most successful debut album in Irish history and reached number two in the UK album chart.

House Music

Invented by the subterranean club DJs of Chicago, this dance music involved an intense, pulsating, often electronic beat sampling in one of its earliest forms. Several different styles of house emerged including acid house, deep house, rap house, hip house and ambient house.

Houston, Whitney

The world was ready for a new 80s soul diva and this 19-year-old gospel singer with a huge voice and wide smile did not disappoint. As the daughter of soul singer Cissy Houston, cousin of Dionne Warwick and goddaughter of Aretha Franklin, her pedigree was solid gold. 'Saving All My Love for You', her 1985 jazzy ballad about a love affair with a married man topped the charts in both the UK and the US and it was the beginning of a stratospheric rise to fame that followed the release of 80s dance floor classic 'I Wanna Dance with Somebody' and the power ballad 'Didn't We Almost Have it All'. Houston was a big supporter of the then imprisoned Nelson Mandela and in 1988 she thrilled British fans by

WHITNEY WITH HER
MUM CISSY HOUSTON.

performing at the Wembley Stadium concert celebrating his 70th birthday. By the end of the decade Whitney was well on her way to selling 150 million records and was ranked the fourth most successful female performer of all time.

Huey Lewis and The News

With the popularity of New Wave and synth pop on the wane by the middle of the decade, pop/rock bands with an upbeat melodious twist began to steal the limelight with Huey and his band mates at the forefront. Creating 'The Power of Love' and 'Back in Time' for the iconic movie *Back to the Future* hurtled this San Francisco pub/rock band into mainstream success winning them an Academy Award and worldwide fame.

Hughes, John

Master of the teen movie, Hughes wrote and directed many of the decade's most influential films aimed at a youthful audience. His list of credits includes *The Breakfast Club*, *Ferris Bueller's Day Off*, and *Pretty in Pink*. His insightful and sensitive, not to say hilarious, look at the turbulent world of the adolescent brilliantly defined the scope of the teenage movie.

Human League, The

Sporting more eyeliner than Cleopatra and the decade's longest fringe, Phil Oakey set teenage hearts aflutter as the lead singer of this pioneering electronic pop band. After spotting two schoolgirls dancing in a Sheffield nightclub in 1980 he asked them to join his band. Joanne Catherall and Susan Ann Sulley added glamour to the line-up and the following year the group released the album *Dare*. Singles 'Love Action' and 'Open Your Heart' charted well but it was the impossibly catchy track 'Don't You Want Me', that was to catapult them into musical history. Oakey had not wanted to release it as a single, believing it was the weakest track on the album, but it went straight to number one, took the coveted Christmas chart-topping slot and sold more than two million copies.

i-D Magazine

The achingly hip fashion and lifestyle magazine was founded by former Vogue art director Terry Jones. Only 40 pages long, the 1980 launch issue was a fanzine for the new street style of post punk London and featured the opinions and musical/fashion tastes of young city dwellers. The magazine includes interviews and features about the hippest names, and nearly every cover shows the star winking and smiling in an emulation of the magazine's logo which shows a winking face if turned on its side – and was first seen 20 years before any text message emoticons.

Idol, Billy

Born William Broad in London, the rocker was branded 'Idle' at school by exasperated teachers. Years later, while choosing a stage name he remembered the tag and resurrected it – this time choosing a more appropriate spelling.

BILLY IDOL

His punk beginnings led to the formation of first band Generation X but after splitting from the group, Idol relocated to New York City. In 1982 he teamed up with guitarist Steve Stevens and that year released his self-titled debut album. Scoring a hit single with 'White Wedding', there was more success to come with 1984's 'Rebel Yell'. His bleached, spiky hair, black leather jacket and sneering good looks appealed to American audiences and his MTV-friendly videos saw them heavily rotated by the music channel. A decline in his success led to addiction problems, rehab and several years where he disappeared off the music radar. In 1996 he staged a comeback after a cameo role playing himself in the 80s nostalgia movie *The Wedding Singer*.

INXS and Michael Hutchence

Fronted by the deeply charismatic Michael Hutchence, the Aussie rockers released their first European single 'Simple Simon/We Are the Vegetables' in France in 1980. Despite this inauspicious start, they went on to become one of the most successful rock bands of all time. They easily filled stadiums, not only with breathless fans whose only desire was to ogle Hutchence, but also with serious music lovers who came to listen to the band's unique blend of new wave/ska and pub rock.

After a succession of successful albums, Hutchence branched out to acting starring in Richard Lowenstein's

INXS FRONTMAN MICHAEL HUTCHENCE.

cult classic *Dogs in Space*. Though their popularity had waned by the end of the decade, Hutchence continued to front INXS until his death in November 1997.

Iranian Embassy Siege

On the evening of May 5 1980 television viewers watching the snooker championships or an old John Wayne film were astonished when the broadcasters suddenly switched to showing a real-life drama taking place in London's Knightsbridge. For the previous six days, five armed terrorists had occupied the Iranian Embassy and held twenty hostages to ransom, demanding the release of political prisoners held in Iran. When the terrorists shot dead the Iranian Press Attaché, who was one of the hostages held inside the embassy, masked members of the SAS stormed the building. They blew out windows with explosives and quickly hunted down the gunmen. One of the men held hostage inside the building was policeman PC Trevor Lock, who tackled the terrorist leader and saved the life of the first SAS trooper to enter the building. Five of the gunmen were killed by the SAS and one survived because he had been shielded by hostages. Until their daring intervention, in full view of the British public, the SAS had always been a shadowy organisation that deliberately kept a very low profile. Suddenly, these anonymous men, who quickly faded from the public eye the moment their job was done, took on the status of national heroes.

Iron Curtain, The

On 5 March 1946, at Fulton, Missouri, Winston Churchill used a phrase when warning the world against communism that became part of the language. He said, 'From Stettin in the Baltic to Trieste in the Adriatic an Iron Curtain has descended across the Continent'.

So, throughout the Cold War, the term 'Iron Curtain' was used to describe the dividing line between the democracies of Western Europe and the Communist bloc to the east.

In 1989 the Soviet Union was finally ousted from the client states they had controlled in Eastern Europe since the end of World War II. With the symbolic destruction of the Berlin Wall in 1989, which was built to prevent East Germans from seeking refuge in the West, the other countries of the Warsaw Pact that lay behind the Iron Curtain threw off their communist rulers. Poland, Czechoslovakia, Rumania, Hungary, Bulgaria, Estonia, Latvia and Lithuania, whose Communist rulers had always obeyed their masters in the Kremlin, declared themselves democracies.

J

Jackson, Janet

Despite always being slightly overshadowed by the phenomenal success of her older brother Michael, Janet Jackson's solo career began to take shape towards the end of the 80s. Shaking off the goody-two shoes image she had cultivated with small roles in the TV shows *Diff'rent Strokes* and *Fame* she broke away from her father's professional control and collaborated with respected R&B producers Jimmy Jam and Terry Lewis to create the album *Control*, which contributed to the rise of a fresh genre of music known as New Jack Swing, a fusion of R&B, funk, rap and disco. The album, which contained the memorable singles 'What Have You Done for Me Lately',

JANET JACKSON ON *DIFF'RENT STROKES.*

'Let's Wait Awhile' and 'When I Think of You', went triple platinum and was lapped up by fans looking for an edgier alternative to the more pop-driven Whitney Houston.

Jackson, Michael

Michael Jackson was already a big star at the start of the 80s but this was the decade in which he rocketed to a new level of completely unprecedented superstardom. It began with *Off the Wall*, his first solo album as an adult, and this superbly crafted set of funky dance tunes and sentimental ballads established Jackson as a mature performer and songwriter. In 1982 Jackson released the Quincy Jones produced album *Thriller* and although the music industry and Jackson fans had been waiting in optimistic anticipation of a smash hit, no-one could foresee just how big it was going to be. The best-selling album of all time, it contained inspired collaborations with Paul McCartney on 'The Girl is Mine' and guitar legend Eddie Van Halen, who added an electrifying solo on 'Beat It'. But drafting in horror movie actor Vincent Price to voice a chilling narration over the title track was the true stroke of genius.

The accompanying video, directed by *American Werewolf in London* creator John Landis, and featuring a demonic Jackson dancing with decaying zombies, was a special-effects masterpiece and revolutionized the music video genre. Jackson solidified his self-proclaimed title as King of Pop when he performed the Moonwalk for the first time in front of an enthralled TV audience of 47 million. Although he admitted that he didn't invent the Moonwalk, it became as closely associated with Jackson as his crotch-grabbing, high-pitched oohs and aahs and his single, sequined, white glove.

With his electrifying success also came a media frenzy and countless stories of Jackson's increasingly bizarre private life began to circulate. These included tales of him sleeping in a hyperbaric chamber and buying the bones of The Elephant Man. Matters were not helped when Jackson was increasingly seen in the company of his pet chimpanzee Bubbles and his face was changing at an alarming due to a seemingly unhealthy use of cosmetic surgery procedures.

Despite now being saddled with the rather dubious nickname of Wacko Jacko, his fans stayed true and he would release *Bad* in 1987, which debuted at Number one, selling eight million copies. Following the 80s Jackson would be blighted with child sex abuse allegations, prescription drug addiction and his eventual death in 2009 from an overdose of powerful sedative drugs. But his legacy as an exceptional music maker remains, as does his undisputed title of King of Pop.

Jive Bunny

For a novelty act fronted by a giant toy rabbit they didn't half do well, selling more than 15 million records. Sampling

ALLY MOLLOY

MICHAEL JACKSON IN *CAPTAIN EO* (1986).

MICHAEL JACKSON IN
HIS PRIME.

music from bygone eras such as Glenn Miller's 'In the Mood' and Bill Haley's 'Rock Around the Clock', they blended these vintage tunes with electronic dance beats creating medleys sure to get people on the dance floor. In just six months in 1989 this act scored three number one singles with 'Swing the Mood', 'That's What I Like' and 'Let's Party' and were one of the first bands to bring 'sampling' into the mainstream charts.

Joel, Billy

Although a successful artist in the US, the 1983 release of 'Uptown Girl' would propel this New York singer song-writer and pianist to worldwide acclaim. Written about his super-model girlfriend Christine Brinkley, whom he later married, the joyful upbeat song told the tale of a simple boy falling for a beautiful woman whose glamorous lifestyle is out of his league. It was said to be Princess Diana's favourite song of the year and when she gave her surprise performance on stage with Wayne Sleep at the Royal Opera house, she chose this track to accompany them. Joel scored a personal and professional triumph when he embarked on an ambitious tour of the Soviet Union in the summer of 1987, becoming the first US rock star to stage a stadium event since the Berlin Wall went up. Joel's success as a live performer and recording artist continued well into the Millennium and he remains the third best-selling solo artist in US history.

John, Elton

Coming out of the 70s as one of the world's biggest stars, this flamboyant performer renewed his songwriting partnership with Bernie Taupin and, thanks to some impressive melodies and sophisticated lyrics, enjoyed early 80s success with singles 'Blue Eyes', 'I'm Still Standing' and 'I Guess That's Why They Call It The Blues' in 1983.

ELTON JOHN AT THE PIANO.

On Valentine's Day the following year fans and music industry insiders were shocked when the star, who had previously been thought of as gay, married a woman! In a lavish ceremony Elton expressed deep love for German-born sound engineer Renate Blauel, but the marriage was to end in divorce four years later. Elton went on to marry his partner David Furnish in a civil partnership ceremony near his Windsor mansion in 2005. Despite many lurid tabloid headlines about his past troubles with drug addiction and eating disorders, Elton is today viewed as a British treasure and has sold more than 250 million records over a remarkable career spanning four decades.

Johnny Hates Jazz

This clean-cut, boys-next-door trio hit the charts with music that reflected their image perfectly. Using rhythm and blues influences, they blended this laid-back sound with the drum machines and tinny pop that were so ubiquitous in the 80s. They named the group after a friend, who really did hate jazz, and had a string of hits following the release of the single 'Shattered Dreams' in 1986 and their number one album *Turn Back the Clock*. The choice of album title proved to be ironic as shortly afterwards chief songwriter Clark Datchler quit and a world tour had to be cancelled. The group eventually replaced him with another vocalist but the JHJ heyday was over.

Jones, Aled

This angelic choirboy became a musical sensation when his version of 'Walking in the Air', taken from the beloved animated film *The Snowman*, landed in the charts in 1985. The nation welcomed this loveable 14-year-old into their hearts and he swapped his life as a Welsh choirboy for fully-fledged celebrity. By the time Aled's voice broke at the age of 16, he had performed for the Queen, the Prince and Princess of Wales and Pope John Paul II and sung at the wedding of hip music celebrities Bob Geldof and Paula Yates. During his short 80s career Aled managed to record 16 albums and sell six million records.

Jones, Grace

Known as much for her severe square-cut hairstyles and striking, androgynous image as her music, the Jamaican-born former model had been a hit on the underground dance music circuit before she broke into the mainstream with her post-disco dance track 'Pull up to the Bumper' in 1981. Grace had a reputation as a diva and this was exemplified when she slapped Russell Harty on his TV chat-show, accusing him of ignoring her. Grace turned this bad girl image to her advantage and won the role of May Day, a villain possessing super-human strength, in the 1985 James Bond movie *A View to a Kill*.

GRACE JONES IN *A VIEW TO KILL* (1985).

Jones, Howard

Along with his trademark cockatoo hairstyle, Jones will be remembered for his blend of new wave/synth pop and upbeat soul music. This classically trained pianist quit the Northern Royal College of Music and swapped the ivory keys for a synthesizer and drum machine. After solo stints in a variety of Southampton clubs, the influential DJ John Peel noticed Jones and offered him a BBC session. The exposure helped win him a record contract and in 1983 he released two singles 'New Song' and 'What is Love' which peaked at number three and number two respectively and he hit the coveted number one spot the following year with his debut album *Human's Lib*.

Just Good Friends

Another hit comedy show from the prolific mind of John Sullivan, who had already created *Citizen Smith* and *Only Fools and Horses* by the time he came to write *Just Good Friends* in 1983. The idea came to him when his wife read out a letter in a newspaper about a woman who had been jilted at the altar. A further spur for the show came from actress Cheryl Hall, who told Sullivan he wrote lousy parts for women in his comedies. Stung by what he perceived as the truth of her remark he deliberately set about crafting a feisty and funny woman character. The result was Penny, played by Jan Francis. Opposite her was Paul Nicholas in the part of Vincent in his first big TV role, although he was already a major star as a singer. The chemistry worked; Penny, as the middle-class girl who was jilted at the altar five years before the action of the storyline begins, is clearly the perfect match for the charming, working-class Jack-the-Lad whose father is a wealthy, rough-hewn, scrap metal dealer with a heart of gold. Sullivan got the romance and the humour just right.

Kajagoogoo

Teen favourites Kajagoogoo released their first single 'Too Shy' in January 1983. Produced by Duran Duran's Nick Rhodes it was followed by two more hits 'Ohh To Be Ahh' and 'Hang On Now' and the number five album *White Feathers*. Previously called Art Nouveau, the band's founding members (Nick Beggs [bass], Steve Askew [guitar], Stuart Croxford Neale [keyboards] and drummer Jez Strode) failed to make any impression until Christopher Hamill, using the stage name Limahl – an anagram of his surname –auditioned as vocalist. Intrigued by word play, the band changed their name to Kajagoogoo, coined when they phonetically wrote out a baby's first words!

Karate Kid, The

An example of the western world's craze for oriental martial arts, this is the likeable 1984 film telling the story of teenager Daniel LaRusso (played by Ralph Macchio) moving with his single-parent mother from New Jersey to California where he feels lonely and cut off from his past. Bullies from the local Karate Club pick on him and he has no way to fight back, until he meets a handyman

THE KARATE KID

called Mr Miyagi, who is also a master of karate, having been taught the skills by his father when he was a boy in his native Okinawa. Mr Miyagi teaches his protégé karate and Ralph enters the Karate Championship to face his old enemy in the final.

Kennedy, Nigel

In the 80s classical musicians were expected by the public to be respectable individuals who led sober lives dedicated to their demanding profession. Nigel Kennedy changed all that. Taking his cue from Mick Jagger, who also grew up in middle-class respectability, Kennedy changed his own gentle speech to the more street-cred vowels of the mockney Jagger. Born in Brighton, Kennedy came from a line of distinguished musicians, as an infant prodigy he went on to study at the Yehudi Menuhin School of Music. Although he has been criticised for his assumption of a punk personality his musical ability is held in the highest regard. Twice married, he is best known by the public for his now famous rendition of Vivaldi's 'The Four Seasons' and his support of Aston Villa football club.

Kensit, Patsy

Though the flaxen-haired Kensit had enjoyed success as a child actress in both TV and film, it was only after she started singing with her big brother Jamie's band Spice in

1983 that she really exploded on to the celebrity scene. The girl from a West London council estate was the daughter of notorious pickpocket, Jimmy the Dip, and counted the Krays as family friends.

After changing the group's name to Eighth Wonder, Patsy and fellow bandmates Jamie Kensit and Geoff Beauchamp on guitar, drummer Jake Walters and Lawrence Lewis playing bass, spent a year gigging around London. The music was considered pretty dire but what they lacked in finesse was more than made up for by Patsy's radiant, golden-girl good looks. Dressed in an array of jewel-coloured, sparkly shift dresses, blonde hair flying, the press became interested (more in the beautiful Kensit than the band) and they were soon signed to CBS Records. It was at one of their early performances that Patsy came to the attention of Steve Wooley, owner of Palace films who was casting for a musical version of Colin McInnis's ode to 1950s youth culture *Absolute Beginners* in which she was offered the role of Crepe Suzette. The movie flopped and Eighth Wonder's small UK success was soon on the wane. Though very popular in Italy and Japan, their only hit record in the UK was 'I'm Not Scared', written by The Pet Shop Boys.

Kensit was not popular with teenage audiences, nor did she help matters by squeaking crassly: 'All I want is to be more famous than anyone and anything.'

Music aside, she continued to act in BBC costume dramas and mostly British-made films. In 1988 she married the first of four husbands (Dan Donovan) and finished the decade starring as Mel Gibson's love interest in *Lethal Weapon 2*.

Kershaw, Nik

Softly-spoken Kershaw ruled the charts in 1984 when he released a series of self-penned hit singles and two top ten albums: *Human Racing* and *The Riddle*. He continued his triumphant chart domination throughout the decade's remainder with a four song set at Live Aid and is responsible for 80s classics 'Wouldn't It Be Good' and 'I Won't Let The Sun Go Down On Me'. Kershaw is considered a songwriter and musician of great stature not only by fans, but also by critics and his peers in the music industry.

Knight Rider

With David 'The Hoff' Hasselhoff as ultimate good guy Michael Knight, *Knight Rider* rode the top of the TV charts from 1982 to 1986. Though 'The Hoff' looked pretty splendid in his shades, open-necked shirts and skin-tight jeans, the real star of the show was a black Pontiac Trans Am called KITT. This car literally had a mind of its own. Fitted with an excess of James Bond-worthy gadgets, KITT's special features were its advanced artificial intelligence and its ability to speak.

KNIGHT RIDER'S CAR 'KITT'

Able to advise, soothe and make clever jokes, KITT (which stood for Knight Industries Two Thousand) was the brainchild of terminally ill, reclusive billionaire Wilton Knight. When cop Michael Long is betrayed by corrupt colleagues, shot through the head and terribly disfigured, he is rescued by the Knight owned FLAG (Foundation For Law And Government) a secret crime fighting organisation. With a face reconstructed to resemble the young and healthy Wilton, Michael Long is resurrected as Michael Knight and paired with KITT to continue their creator's battle with evil. Michael never had to climb stairs as KITT would simply eject him to the desired location; he never carried a gun, instead using his superior fighting skills to overcome the deadliest armed assailants. Always coming out on top, the man/machine duo would speed into the sunset leaving viewers feeling all was right with the world

Krankies, The

This weird Scottish comedy duo were made up of Wee Jimmy Krankie, a cheeky 10-year-old schoolboy and his long-suffering father Ian. Stalwarts of 80s prime time television, they presented kids' show *Crackerjack* and had two TV series of their own, *The Krankies Klub* in 1982 and 1985's *The Krankies Electronic Komic*. Wee Jimmy cavorted into all kinds of mischief whilst his dad tried to keep up with the rascal's pranks. Sometimes, Jimmy was disturbingly portrayed as a ventriloquist's dummy. No performance was complete without Jimmy chortling his catch phrase, 'Fan'dabi'dozi' whilst giving a thumbs up to the audience. Oddly, their single of the same name failed to make it past number 46 in the UK charts! Of course the pair were really a middle-aged, married couple called Janette and Ian Tough. Janette's diminutive 4.6in frame enabled her to impersonate a small schoolboy with spooky accuracy. Now semi- retired, they still make occasional TV appearances and are Christmas pantomime favourites.

Labyrinth

Despite its dazzling pedigree – it was directed by Jim Henson, produced by George Lucas and starred David Bowie, who also wrote the songs – *Labyrinth* was not a box office success when it was released in 1986. But over the years it has acquired cult status and has a devoted legion of admirers. A fantasy that brilliantly combines human actors with puppets it is guaranteed to enchant children for generations to come.

Lauper, Cyndi

This vibrant, unique performer was making a statement about 'Girl Power' way before the Spice Girls. The release

OLD MEETS
NEW, CYNDI
LAUPER WITH
LADY GAGA.

of her first album *She's So Unusual* in 1983 gave us the hit single 'Girls Just Want to Have Fun'. It reached number two in both the US and UK charts and soon reached anthem status for a generation of young women tired of the militant women's lib stance of the late 1970's. Lauper's dyed orange hair, colourful clothing and quirky personality alongside kooky statements delivered in a broad New York accent endeared her to the public and helped her achieve superstar status. In spring 1984 follow up single, 'Time After Time' went straight to number one in the US and number 3 in the UK. An autobiographical video accompanied the release featuring appearances by her real life mum and boyfriend. Her success continued throughout the following years with more great records including the beautiful 'True Colours', considered by many as one of the best pop songs ever written.

Laurie, Hugh

James Hugh Calum Laurie was born on 11 June 1959. The son of a doctor who won a gold medal in the 148 Olympic Games for rowing, Laurie went to Eton and then Cambridge University, where he also excelled in rowing, winning a blue in the 1980 Boat Race. A spell of glandular fever ended his rowing career, so he joined Footlights, the Cambridge club that started the career of many actors and comedians. There he met Emma Thompson, with whom he had a brief romance. They remained good friends and it was she who introduced him to his future comedy partner, Stephen Fry.

In 1980/81, his final year at Cambridge, he was president of Footlights with Emma Thompson as vice-president. They took the annual revue, The Cellar Tapes, to the Edinburgh Festival and won the first Perrier Comedy Award. The cast also included Stephen Fry, who co-wrote the show with Laurie, and Emma Thompson, Tony Slattery, Paul Shearer and Penny Dwyer. Success in *Blackadder* and the sketch show *A Bit of Fry and Laurie*. Apart from his brilliant comedy work, Laurie is also a gifted straight actor.

Despite his great and continuing professional success, Hugh Laurie suffers from occasional bouts of clinical depression for which he receives treatment from a psychotherapist.

Less than Zero

The first novel by author Brett Easton Ellis, *Less than Zero* was published in 1985 when the author was just 21 years old. One of the most widely read pop fiction books of the era, the plot follows Clay, an East Coast college student who returns to his home in LA for the Christmas holidays. With Clay initially embarking on a heady round of casual sex and non-stop partying, we learn of his confusing on/off romance with ex-girlfriend Blair and become familiar with the dissolute, over-privileged friends he left behind. With growing unease we witness their jaded reaction to several nightmarish scenarios and see Clay beginning to question the amoral, pointless lifestyle he once embraced. Showing the dark side of early 80s Los Angeles, *Less Than Zero* was also made into a movie of the same name starring Andrew McCarthy and Robert Downey Jr.

Live Aid

On 13 July 1985, Bob Geldof's campaign to save the famine stricken people of Ethiopia culminated in the biggest live concert the world had ever seen. Originally planned as an offshoot from Geldof and Midge Ure's Band Aid project, they had hoped to raise £1 million for Ethiopian famine relief. As plans gathered speed one concert became two with the idea of staging them in London and Philadelphia. More and more countries followed suit and soon Australia, Japan, Austria, the Netherlands, Yugoslavia, Russia, Germany and Norway joined an international satellite network.

Kicking off at 12 noon London time, 7 am in Philadelphia, the gig lasted 16 hours in all. Performers included:

London

Status Quo, The Style Council, The Boomtown Rats, Adam Ant, Ultravox, Spandau Ballet, Elvis Costello, Nik Kershaw, Sade, Sting and Phil Collins, Howard Jones,

Bryan Ferry, Paul Young, Alison Moyet, U2, Dire Straits, Queen, David Bowie, The Who, Elton John, Kiki Dee, George Michael, Andrew Ridgeley, Sir Paul McCartney, Band Aid.

Philadelphia

Joan Baez, The Hooters, The Four Tops, Billy Ocean, Black Sabbath, Run-D.M.C., Rick Springfield, REO Speedwagon, Crosby, Stills and Nash & Young, Judas Priest, Bryan Adams, The Beach Boys, George Thorogood and the Destroyers, Bo Diddley, Simple Minds, The Pretenders, Santana, Ashford & Simpson, Madonna, Tom Petty and the Heartbreakers, Kenny Loggins, The Cars, Neil Young, Power Station, Thompson Twins, Eric Clapton, Led Zeppelin, Duran Duran, Patti LaBelle, Phil Collins (after performing at Wembley he flew to the USA by Concorde) Hall & Oates, Mick Jagger, Tina Turner, Bob Dylan, Keith Richards, Ronnie Wood, USA for Africa.

Lloyd Cole and the Commotions

This indie-style band met as students at the University of Glasgow and achieved cult status in both the UK and the United States. Quoting Bob Dylan and Booker T and the MGs as major influences, their first album *Rattlesnakes* was frequently compared to the work of 1960s group The Velvet Underground.

Philosophy undergraduate Cole thrilled brainy and

precocious teenagers everywhere, not only with his dark stubble, moody eyes and sad half smile, but also with slightly pretentious lyrics referencing Simone de Beauvoir, Norman Mailer and Truman Capote. Guitarist Neil Clark's complicated solos perfectly enhanced Cole's clever lyrics. Other band members including bass guitarist Lawrence Donegan, keyboard player Blair Cowan and Stephen Irvine on drums added to the Commotions' bohemian image.

Lost Boys, The

In 1987 the young Kiefer Sutherland made an outstanding appearance as the vampire leader David in a new interpretation of the legend of the deathless bloodsuckers. When two brothers move to a new town inhabited by a gang of bikers, they learn of the strange deaths that have been taking place. Then the older brother starts to shows signs of being a vampire, so the younger brother recruits two vampire hunters and goes to war. Director Joel Schumacher dared to break away from the time-trusted formula and play some of the horror for laughs.

COREY FELDMAN AND COREY HAIM IN *THE LOST BOYS*

Madonna

In 1982 the 24-year-old Madonna signed a contract with Sire Records. Two years later she'd had three minor dance hits and her first top five record, 'Lucky Star' was climbing the US billboard charts. In November 'Like a Virgin' reached Number one in four countries.

Madonna had spent the summer of 1984 filming a small part in the Susan Seidelmen-directed movie, *Desperately Seeking Susan*, a vehicle for successful actress Rosanna Arquette.

The film was released in 1985 and Madonna stole the show. She also sold millions of records, toured America and met bad boy actor Sean Penn, whom she married

MADONNA

after a whirlwind love affair. The marriage was stormy and not helped by the release of nude photographs and a soft porn movie made during her early years in New York.

In January 1986 the couple, now dubbed the 'Poison Penns' flew to Hong Kong to film the disastrous *Shanghai Surprise*. Their publicist resigned after two days and on-set rumours of bitter arguments, heavy drinking and dramatic tantrums were leaked to the press.

Despite the trouble in her marriage, Madonna's career kept getting stronger and new album *True Blue* topped the charts in 28 countries. In 1987 she made the comedy '*Who's That Girl?*' a box-office flop that was panned by critics and avoided by the public, yet her world tour of the same name was a sell out success. In 1989 Madonna and Sean Penn divorced. More positively, she is paid $5 million to advertise Pepsi in a television commercial that will also promote her new single, 'Like a Prayer'.

The ad was broadcast on the same day in 40 countries to an audience of 250 million. Sentimental and sweet, the commercial involves a dreamy Madonna stepping back in time to meet her eight-year-old self and poignantly wandering through her childhood home. We also see her happily dancing in the street with her new record playing in the background.

The following day when the singer's own video premiered on MTV things were a little different.

This version saw a scantily clad Madonna dancing amidst

a ring of burning crosses, an emblem of notorious American racist group the Ku Klux Klan. In another she kisses an African/American model dressed as Jesus and then caresses herself whilst writhing on a chapel pew.

Uproar ensued as the ex-convent schoolgirl was accused of ridiculing Christianity. Enraged protest groups demanded Pepsi end their contract with her, religious leaders including a Catholic bishop cried for a boycott of not just Pepsi but all their other business holdings. The Vatican then stepped in, causing more shock waves when the Pope called for her to be banned from performing in Italy. Bowing to pressure Pepsi dropped the ad and the sponsorship deal. Professing mild surprise at the international scandal, Madonna had received billions of dollars in free publicity, her name mentioned on almost every news channel in the world. It would prove priceless for her career.

'Like a Prayer' went to number one in 30 different countries. People who would never have known her name bought the record. She also kept the $5 million Pepsi advance.

By New Years Eve 1989 she was the most written about, photographed woman in the world apart from Diana, Princess of Wales. She epitomised the 'know what you want then grab it' consciousness of the time.

Madness

The ska revivalists spent a total of 214 weeks in the UK charts during the 80s. They were the opening act on the first *Top of the Pops* of the decade performing their number three hit 'My Girl'. With their joyful melodies and cheeky chappy personas the seven-man line-up were favourites on TV as well as legendary live performers. Fronted by lead singer Suggs, they were nicknamed the

MADNESS

'Nutty Boys' by fans who were delighted to see saxophonist Lee Thomson fly through the air on wires for his solo in the video of the delightful ode to schooldays, 'Baggy Trousers'. In spite of the feel-good factor in many of their songs, the band's records often hid a gritty social comment, with 'Embarrassment' dealing with a family's reaction to a teenager's pregnancy and 'House of Fun' referring to a boy's attempts to buy condoms on his sixteenth birthday.

Malcolm McLaren

The impresario who gave the world punk also introduced the UK to Hip-Hop culture, break-dancing and the then unheard method of 'record scratching' with 1982 hit Buffalo Gals.

Mandela, Nelson

On 1 January 1980 Nelson Mandela was serving his 16th year in prison. He had been a leading figure in the battle against apartheid. A political activist since university days, he had joined the National African Congress (ANC) in 1944 and helped found its youth league. After studying law, he and fellow activist Oliver Tambo opened South Africa's first black-owned law firm.

In 1960, after police shot and killed 200 unarmed protestors and the government banned the ANC,

NELSON MANDELA
WITH DIANA ROSS.

Mandela, who had previously adhered to a strict non-violent ethos began to advocate acts of sabotage and became a fugitive. Captured in 1962, he was serving a five-year jail term when a charge of treason, sabotage and violent conspiracy led to the further sentence of life imprisonment.

In 1980, the now exiled Oliver Tambo began a campaign to free Mandela. Worldwide, sanctions against the country were tightened and soon the era's biggest stars lent their support.

70th Birthday Concert

As his 70th birthday and 25th year of captivity approached, plans were made to hold a celebratory concert that would be televised and raise consciousness about apartheid. Staged on 11 June 1988 at London's Wembley Stadium the line up included:

Sting, Harry Belafonte, George Michael, Lenny Henry, Sir Richard Attenborough, Whoopi Goldberg, Richard Gere, Eurhythmics, Al Green, Joe Cocker, Freddie Jackson, Ashford & Simpson, Fry & Laurie, Tracy Chapman, Joan Armatrading, Tony Hadley, Midge Ure, Phil Collins, Paul Young, Bryan Adams, Bee Gees, Natalie Cole, Jackson Brown, Aswad, Sly & Robbie, Simple Minds, Johnny Marr, Peter Gabriel, Harry Enfield, Whitney Houston, Chubby Checker, Billy Connolly, Dire Straits, Salt-N-Pepa, Jessie Norman and a surprise slot by Stevie Wonder.

As the decade closed, Mandela was still a prisoner. He finally walked free on February 11 1990.

Maradona's Hand of God

Probably the most infamous goal ever 'scored' against an English team was allowed when Maradona handled the ball during the 1986 FIFA World Cup quarter-final. The Argentinean claimed that the foul, not seen by the referee but recorded by the camera, was 'a little with the head of Maradona and a little with the hand of God.' What is now virtually forgotten in England is that Maradona, later in the match, went on to beat six English defenders and score what was voted by FIFA officials as the Goal of the Century.

Marilyn

Born Peter Robinson in Kingston, Jamaica, he was a popular 'face' amongst London's hippest set and shared a squat with Boy George. The cross-dresser based his look on sex bomb Marilyn Monroe and came to public attention via an appearance in a Eurythmics video. His only hit, 'Calling Your Name', was released in 1983.

Mel & Kim

Chirpy sisters Melanie and Kim Appleby grew up in London's East End and owed their stunning good looks to their mixed English and Jamaican parentage. Spotted dancing in a nightclub they were quickly contracted to Supreme records and produced by Stock, Aitken and Waterman. Launched under the name Mel & Kim, they went to number three with first release 'Showing Out (Get Fresh at The Weekend)' and number one on both sides of the Atlantic with 'Respectable'. The girls were popular for their unique look, mixing urban street wear with high fashion and were headed for global stardom.

In 1987, just as their album *F.L.M.* was released, tragedy struck as Mel was diagnosed with cancer of the spine. She had beaten the disease once already, prior to their success; it had been kept a secret from fans. She withdrew from public life to concentrate on her treatment, finally passing away in 1990. She was 23.

Miami Vice

Sometimes a series comes along and changes everything. So it was with *Miami Vice* when it started in 1984. Apart from the fast-paced, sharp-edged scripts, producer Michael Mann was determined to bring major movie values to the show and dazzle the viewers with the stunning, semi-tropical locations. From the fabulous shimmering beaches to the palm-lined boulevards, where glorious Art Deco hotels glowed in the neon lit darkness, Miami vice had a look that could not be matched by competitors. Even the streets were specially watered for

MIAMI VICE

night scenes so they always glittered. Then there were the stars. Don Johnson as Detective 'Sonny' Crockett with his partner Detective Ricardo Tubbs, played by Phillip Michael Thomas, were the definition of cool. Designer clothes and bags of attitude set an unmatched style in leading men. And there was the music. From the moment you heard Jan Hammer's *Miami Vice* theme pounding out you knew you were in for a musical treat, Phil Collins, Glen Frey, Peter Gabriel and U2 all contributed over the years. Despite the glamour, the show did not turn away from the dark underside of the city, where fortunes in drug money attracted the vicious and corrupt.

Michael, George, and Wham!

At 19, along with his childhood friend Andrew Ridgeley, George Michael burst onto the music scene in 1982 as the lead singer of Wham!

With sunbed tans and home-dyed highlights they belted out hits such as 'Club Tropicana' and 'Wake Me Up Before You Go Go', symbolizing the feel good factor of the 80s. Feeding their screaming teenage fans a diet of catchy, saccharine pop, whilst dancing around in Choose Life T-shirts and micro-shorts, Wham! became one of the best-selling bands of the decade churning out three hit albums. Michael described the time as 'magical' but admitted that although he was confident in his song writing abilities, he desperately wanted to leave the heart-throb imagery to Ridgeley because he felt like a fake. Breaking ground the band toured China in 1985 and appeared alongside Elton John at the Live Aid concert.

But four years after it had started it was all over. Michael's triumphant solo release of 'Careless Whisper' and his desire to cultivate a more sophisticated image and attract an older audience than their most teenage fan-base led to the duo parting amicably. But not before staging an historic, farewell concert at Wembley Stadium called 'Wham! The Final'.

GEORGE MICHAEL, LEAD SINGER OF WHAM!

Whilst Michael, who had written virtually all the Wham! songs, released his first solo album *Faith* to great critical acclaim in 1987 and went on to become one of the world's most admired and successful singer songwriters, Ridgeley would move to Monaco and try his hand at Formula Three motor racing with far less success.

Milli Vanilli

They sparked one of the biggest scandals in pop music history when it was revealed that the strikingly handsome pair had not sung a note on the multiple platinum album *All or Nothing* (released as *Girl You Know It's True* in the USA).

The German Svengali behind the debacle, Frank Farian, had already found vocalists for the record, but deciding the real singers had the wrong image he recruited models Rob Pilatus and Fabrice Morvan whom he had spotted in a Berlin nightclub. The secret was revealed when a tape the models were lip-syncing to jammed during a 'live' performance for MTV. With the same line repeating itself over and over, Rob and Fab dropped microphones and ran off the stage in fright. Weirdly, fans did not seem to notice or comprehend the significance of the incident, but critics did and after Farian confessed his ploy to the press, the boys had to return their Grammy award and disappeared into humiliated obscurity.

Minder

Veteran scriptwriter Leon Griffiths created this popular show, basing the character of Terry McCann, played by Denis Waterman, on a real life villain's bodyguard. The star was George Cole, as Arthur Daley, the man who put the phrase ''er indoors,' on the lips of the nation's married men and became one of the comedy immortals of the 80s's. Originally produced by Verity Lambert, the hour-long show usually involved Arthur getting the easy-going Terry into some less-than-legal situation that he would often have to solve with his fists. The two leading characters were brilliantly drawn, with Arthur filled with social pretensions, forever planning a business empire from his lock-up premises, and uncomplicated, kind-hearted Terry always ready to have the wool pulled over his eyes, despite all the previous trouble he'd been landed in by Arthur's double dealings. Much of the action took place in the Winchester Club, presided over by the affable Dave, a place where the local police would often drop in to visit the odd couple.

Minogue, Kylie

With perhaps prophetic irony, the tiny pop princess trilled 'I Should Be So Lucky' and found a colossal career that's still going strong. Cute as a button Kylie, just signed to Australia's Mushroom Records, travelled to the UK to work with producers Stock, Aitken and Waterman. They

ALLY MOLLOY

KYLIE MINOGUE

had forgotten she was coming and famously wrote 'I Should Be So Lucky' there and then while Kylie languished outside the studio, and she then laid down her vocals in less than an hour. The unimagined chart success that followed inspired Mike Stock to travel to Australia where Kylie was back at work on *Neighbours* to apologise for initially forgetting about her. He then convinced her to return to London and record her debut album, *Kylie*. Suddenly it was Kylie mania; the public were besotted. The schoolgirl's favourite was not only a gay icon but many teenage boys' ideal too and 18 years on the love story continues.

Moonlighting

Created by Glenn Gordon Caron and first broadcast in 1986, *Moonlighting* saved the faltering career of Cybill Shepherd and launched Bruce Willis onto the first stage of superstardom. With a hit theme song sung by Al Jarreau, this brilliant series plotted the adventures of Maddie Hayes, played by Cybill Shepherd, and Bruce Willis as David Addison, who were the sole employees of the Blue Moon detective agency. The plots were a cleverly woven mixture of comedy, drama and romance, but the real point of the show was the sexual tension between the two stars and the ever-present question, will they or won't they ever make love? On the long journey to the inevitable, the dialogue crackled with wisecracks, brilliant one-liners and constant references to the classic movies of the past as well as other famous TV detectives. Always funny, sharp and clever, the overlapping dialogue was delivered at a sizzling pace and has seldom been equalled by other shows.

Moore, Demi

Born in Roswell, New Mexico, Demi Moore came to prominence at the age of twenty-two in movies like *St Elmo's Fire* and *About Last Night*. She had survived an unstable childhood: her parents were both alcoholics and the family moved frequently, eventually settling in Los Angeles, where Demi attended the same high school as actor Timothy Hutton. Her eyes are different colours, a condition known as heterochromia, one being green and the other hazel. She was cross-eyed as a girl until surgery finally corrected the problem; she also suffered from a kidney dysfunction. Despite her health she went on to be one of the most successful and highly paid women in Hollywood.

MTV

Short for Music Television, MTV began broadcasting on 1 August 1981, when the words 'Ladies and gentlemen, rock and roll' were spoken by John Lack. Originally founded to play music videos, presented by 'VJs', the

DEMI MOORE IN THE 1982 MOVIE *PARASITE*.

channel proved to be a massive success with the young and its influence on contemporary pop culture cannot be measured. The first video ever shown on the channel was the appropriately titled 'Video Killed the Radio Star', by The Buggles.

Musical Youth

The Birmingham-born quintet was quite a novelty in 1982 due to their young ages – they were between 12 and 16 years old. The British/Jamaican band were signed to MCA records and saw first release 'Pass the Dutchie' go to Number one in the United Kingdom and several other countries worldwide. Started by brothers Junior (drums) and Patrick Waite (bass) under the guidance of their musician father, Freddie, they were soon joined by family friends and brothers Kelvin (guitar) and Michael (keyboard) Grant. With singer Dennis Seaton added to the mix, Musical Youth was born.

Though 'Pass the Dutchie' sold over 4 million copies and the kids were nominated for a Grammy award, even a duet with Donna Summer failed to keep them on top and they split in 1984.

N

Neighbours

In 1986 Britain was hit by an Australian juggernaut in the form of *Neighbours*. This daytime soap became a national phenomenon with Kylie Minogue, Jason Donovan and Craig McLachlan riding on its tidal wave of success. Centred on the residents of Ramsay Street, a middle-class cul de sac in the fictional Melbourne suburb of Erinsborough, UK audiences, which frequently hit more than 14 million, couldn't get enough. The nation was gripped by the romance of Scott and Charlene – played by superstars Jason and Kylie – and such was the excitement that surrounded their on-screen marriage, tabloids likened it to the wedding of Charles and Diana.

ALLY MOLLOY

NEIGHBOURS

Storylines featuring other characters such as the street's resident busybody Mrs Mangel, widower Jim Robinson, his ruthless businessman son Paul, glamorous granny Helen Daniels and the pompous Harold Bishop kept the country hooked. The soap, where every day seemed to be blessed with clear-blue skies, was in stark contrast to the more gritty and drab settings of *EastEnders* and *Coronation Street*, also spawned a string of top ten hits with many cast members including Minogue and Donovan pursuing pop careers in the UK.

New Kids on the Block

This group of wannabe bad boys had big hair, big dance routines and even bigger egos. As one of the first manufactured groups of the 80s, they were put together by Maurice Starr who had guided the early success of R&B act New Edition and was looking for a white counterpart to rival them. More than 500 hopefuls came to audition in Boston, where Starr was immediately impressed by 15 year-old Donnie Wahlberg's rapping and dancing and recruited him on the spot. Wahlberg was then instrumental in helping Starr chose the rest of the band, pushing forward his school friends Danny Wood and brothers Jordan and Jonathan Knight. Relentless dance and vocal rehearsals began 1986 but the bland bubblegum pop and formation street dancing failed to make an impact for almost two years and their record company considered

NEW KIDS ON
THE BLOCK

dropping them. After an image rethink they released their second album, *Hangin' Tough*, which reflected their new style. The band embarked on a country wide promotional tour which caught the attention of radio stations and MTV and soon The Kids were being chased in the street by lovesick teenage girls with the album selling millions and eventually turning eight times platinum. This established the boys firmly on their way to worldwide success and hit after hit followed.

New Order

This post-punk electronic dance band was formed in 1980 by the remaining members of Joy Division following the suicide of front man and vocalist Ian Curtis. Curtis took his own life on the eve of an American tour leaving the remaining members, Peter Hook, Stephen Morris and Bernard Sumner devastated. They had previously agreed that the band would not continue should any one member leave, so they honored their pact and dissolved the band. The early output of New Order was overshadowed by the tragic events surrounding their previous incarnation but on upon visiting New York in 1981 they immersed themselves in the City's club scene and became heavily influenced by Latin freestyle and electro dance music. Their 1983 single, 'Blue Monday', was a departure from their previous work and is seen as one of the most important crossover tracks of the 80s pop scene. Blending dance beats with synthesized instrumentation it stands out as the first British dance track to exhibit an obvious influence from the New York club scene and remains the best-selling 12-inch of all time.

Newton-John, Olivia

Of all the questionable fashion crazes that were embraced in the 80s the neon-coloured sports headband was one of the most unflattering. And we have this fresh-faced Australian actress and singer to thank. Following her transformation from virginal school-girl to sex siren in the smash hit musical *Grease*, Olivia was keen to shake off her girl-next door image and released the album *Physical* in 1981. The lyrics to the title track were deemed overly suggestive and to counteract this she filmed a tongue-in-cheek video to accompany it portraying the singer in skin-tight spandex sporting the soon to be ubiquitous headband.

New Wave

It's difficult to pin down exactly what made up this fresh genre of music and style because the term was very loosely used to define almost every band that sprung up at the beginning of the decade. Essentially, its roots began in the late 70s post-punk era. Although the bands were still deemed rebellious and alternative the songs were more tuneful and less raw than the haphazard and anarchic offerings of their predecessors. Relying heavily on synthesizers and influenced by the more melodic sounds of disco and 1960s pop, New Wave had hit the mainstream by 1980 and began to dominate the charts.

Whilst bands such as Blondie and The Human League presented more polished and alluring images there was a darker side to the New Wave movement epitomized by groups like The Cure, Siouxsie and Banshees and The Smiths. Their music was more tortured and self-expressive, as was the fashion style, which was deliberately unglamorous, with ghoulish make-up and macabre, ill-fitting clothes.

Although it was an experimental time, the New Wave movement's early use of electronic dance beats, synthesized orchestration and melodic vocals are seen as direct influences on the house and techno music revolutions that were yet to come.

9½ Weeks

One of those films of 1986 that everyone heard of but not so many actually went to see. In the United States it only grossed $7 million and was dismissed by the critics. It enjoyed a bigger reputation in Europe for its erotic sadomasochistic content. There is little to the plot, Mickey Rourke takes the part of a Wall Street executive, John Grey, and Kim Basinger plays Elizabeth McGraw, who works in an art gallery. Over the 9½ weeks of the title they explore a variety of dangerous sexual games that ultimately leads to her breaking down and leaving him.

Gary Numan

Whilst later 80s electronic/synth pop acts would concentrate on more cheerful, upbeat brands of chart-topper, Numan's lyrics and style reflected the teenage angst-ridden dilemmas of unrequited love, alienation and insecurity. Sometimes referred to as 'the lonely android', Numan cultivated a reclusive, almost robotic image and was a driven and creative loner. His 1980 songs, including 'We Are Glass' and 'I Die, You Die' touched a chord with the more sensitive and anguished in society and his armies of loyal and devoted fans were known as 'Numanoids.' By the following year, weary from the pressures of fame and exposure, he announced his retirement and staged a series of farewell concerts at Wembley Arena. Numan recalled later in his biography that he stood on an empty stage following the final concert and thought: 'What the f★★★ have I done?' Numan's music left a huge legacy and was the inspiration for many electronic bands that followed him earning his the erstwhile moniker 'The Godfather of Techno'.

O'Connor, Hazel

Being chosen to play Kate, the lead character in the critically acclaimed movie *Breaking Glass*, propelled this Coventry born performer into the 80s Hall of Fame. The movie chronicled the rise and fall of a young New Wave singer trying to make it big in the music industry. Seen as a groundbreaking movie of its time and exposing a dark, exploitative side of the business, it earned O'Connor a Best Newcomer BAFTA nomination. She scored several hits taken from the movie's soundtrack including 'Eighth Day' and the haunting 'Will You'. When O'Connor toured Britain to promote the album she chose a then unknown act to support her ... Duran Duran. It gave them the exposure they needed to secure a record contract. Although O'Connor recorded several follow up albums she became disillusioned with the music industry and claimed that she had been 'ripped off, torn up and spat out by the machinery of "Showbiz"'. Hazel possessed a cheery personality and is remembered fondly for her heyday but she was never able to achieve the stratospheric success or longevity of the band she gave a break to three decades ago.

OMD

If their long-winded, full name of Orchestral Manoeuvres in the Dark seemed a tad pretentious we should be grateful that they changed it from their original choice, VCLXI. Silly names aside, this innovative band, formed by Andy McCluskey and Paul Humphreys, had originally been inspired by the experimental electronic music of German bands such as Kraftwerk and Neu. Forming their own brand of catchy, electronic melodies teamed with intelligent lyrics, OMD earned a reputation as the thinking person's pop band particularly after the release of the 1980 hit 'Enola Gay', a wistful, anti-war song named after the plane which dropped the first atomic bomb on the Japanese city of Hiroshima. Their biggest success 'Architecture and Morality' contained the three huge singles; the religiously themed 'Joan of Arc' and 'Maid of Orleans' and the harmonious and choral inspired 'Souvenir'.

Only Fools and Horses

In 1981 the nation was introduced to Derek 'Del Boy' Trotter, his younger brother Rodney and their grandfather, who lived in a high rise flat in Peckham and spent most of their nights in the Nag's Head with the rest of the local lads. Written by John Sullivan, who also composed the theme song for the show, the long-running saga told the story of the two brothers scraping a living from their market stall by selling dodgy items that had usually fallen off the back of a lorry. Although there is always underlying affection, the tension between the two brothers comes from their completely different characters. Del Boy is the eternal optimist who is convinced their fortune will be made by his latest business scam. Rodney is pessimistic and yearns for a more fulfilling life. Over the series we saw the grandfather replaced by Uncle Albert, Rodney marry Cassandra, the daughter of a successful local businessman, and Del marry middle-class Raquel and became a father. Eventually the show was so popular its audience for one Christmas episode was 24.3 million viewers.

Personal Computers

For a long time after the introduction of the computer the idea of an individual having their own personal equipment instead of sharing a main frame with multiple users seemed an unrealisable dream. But such was the speed of the development of microprocessors through the 70s that by the 80s it was suddenly possible for ordinary members of the public to afford a PC. The public were beginning to take for granted incredible advances in tools for communication, entertainment and design.

Pet Shop Boys

After a chance encounter in a London electronics shop in 1981, journalist Neil Tennant and architectural student Chris Lowe combined their mutual interest in dance music and began writing their own. Although much of the public were not to become familiar with their compositions for a good three years it was during this era that the duo penned some of their greatest hits including 'Rent', 'It's a Sin' and 'Jealousy'. In 1983, Tennant, who was writing for music mag *Smash Hits*, was sent to New York to interview The Police, and he used the opportunity to have lunch with New York Hi-NRG producer Bobby 'O'. At this meeting Bobby 'O' suggested making 'West End Girls' after listening to a demo tape Tennant had taken with him. Although a minor success in American clubs the track did not do well in the UK. Undeterred, the boys re-recorded it with synth guru Stephen Hague and it hit the number one spot in nine countries including the UK. Three more number ones followed from the smash hit album *Actually*, with the 80s electro dance classic cover 'Always on My Mind', 'It's a Sin', and 'What Have I Done to Deserve This', a duet between Tennant and the 60s icon Dusty Springfield. At the 2009 Brit Awards the Pet Shop Boys were honoured with an Outstanding Contribution to Music award.

Phoenix, River

Named after the 'river of life' by his free-living hippy parents, River was hailed as one of the most promising young actors of his generation in 1986. Angelic as a child actor, he matured into an exceptionally handsome young man and his gentle personality and superior acting skills captured the attention film directors, critics and film fans alike. First coming to prominence in the Rob Reiner coming-of-age movie *Stand by Me*, the animal rights supporter and strict vegan starred in a string of movie successes in the late 80s including *Indiana Jones and the Last Crusade* in which he played the young Indie, and *Running on Empty* for which he was Oscar nominated as Best Supporting Actor. Possessing a clean-living image and a career heading sky high, River's death from a drug overdose on Halloween 1993 came as a terrible shock.

Phone Cards

Phone cards were greeted with delight when they were introduced in the 80s, as the public suddenly no longer needed to have enough change on them to make an urgent call. Phone cards proved one of the welcome developments brought about by new technology. Parents could also ensure that their children always had the means on them to make a call home.

RIVER PHOENIX

Platoon

This was the 1986 movie that caused America to finally bare its soul in the aftermath of the Vietnam conflict. Director Oliver Stone, who actually fought in the war, saw his sometimes-autobiographical account of the horror receive three Oscars for best director, best editing and best picture. The three stars are Tom Berenger, William Defoe and Charlie Sheen. The story, starring Berenger, Willem Defoe and Charlie Sheen is a simple morality tale of how war dehumanises men and battle leaves nothing but scar tissue on the human heart. It is a universal message, but more painful for Americans who saw their country torn apart by the conflict when it was no longer possible to tell who were the villains and who the heroes.

Police, The

Before frontman Sting went off to achieve major success as a solo artist, The Police would enjoy international acclaim as a new wave rock trio. Vocalist Sting, with Andy Summers on guitar and Stewart Copeland on drums, kicked off 1980 with a world tour, even playing India, Mexico and Egypt, lands that rarely hosted foreign performers. The following year they released *Ghost in the Machine*, an album rich with keyboard and saxophone melodies which spawned the hit singles 'Every Little Thing She Does is Magic' and 'Spirits in the Material World'. As Sting was also stretching his legs as an actor and becoming a major star in his own right, relations with band founder Stuart Copeland became strained and the band were to record their final album *Synchronicity* in 1983. Containing the memorable tracks 'Every Breath You Take' and 'Wrapped Around Your Finger,' it sold extremely well and although they followed this up with a live tour the band was to dissolve shortly afterwards.

Poltergeist

A new type of haunted house movie came in 1982 from a story by Steven Spielberg, who was also one of the writers. Only this time it wasn't a menacing old ruin set in a tangled wasteland, but a spanking new suburban house inhabited by normal, everyday folks. Unbeknown to the Feeling family, the property developers have built their new home on ancient burial grounds and the spirits don't like it. The German word poltergeist means a mischievous ghost that throws things about, and that's only the start of it. At first it's a bit of fun. Kitchen chairs slide about and apparently rearrange themselves; objects begin to whirl around in the air. The real danger comes from the television set. Left on at night when a channel ceases broadcasting the spirit world use it as a means of kidnapping the Feeling family's youngest daughter Carol Ann and drawing her into the ether with them.

Luckily, the Feelings are aided by a tiny woman medium that rescues the child, but the haunted house is utterly destroyed.

Pretenders, The

Chrissie Hynde and her band mates hold the honour of scoring the very first number one of the decade. Hynde disliked the track 'Brass in Pocket' and told her producers to release it 'over my dead body.' Fortunately they ignored her, and Hynde later admitted to feeling rather sheepish at its success. Originally a foursome, two of The Pretenders, James Honeyman-Scott and Peter Farndon, died of drug overdoses leaving just Hynde and drummer Martin Chambers. Hynde carried on with the band that would go through an ever-changing lineup of musicians and released two more albums in the 80s: *Learning to Crawl* and *Get Close* and scoring Top Ten hits with 'Don't Get Me Wrong' and 'Hymn to Her'.

Pretty in Pink

This 80s re-working of the Cinderella story features Molly Ringwald as Andie, a young girl from the wrong side of the tracks, who falls for rich guy Blane, played by heartthrob Andrew McCarthy. Directed by teenage film legend John Hughes, the film has no real surprises but its charm and sensitive depiction of adolescent insecurities

JAMES HONEYMAN-SCOTT OF THE PRETENDERS.

and exceptionally nostalgic soundtrack struck a chord with the youth of the 80s. Andie, a poor but a fashion-conscious student has the misfortune to attend a school that has its more than fair share of snobby, rich kids. Attracted to Blane, who seems kinder than his posh friends, she is thrilled when he asks her to the Senior Prom, only for him to retract the invitation when he falls foul of peer pressure. Andie's knight in shining armour is Duckie, her geeky childhood friend, played with immense charm by Jon Cryer. Duckie, along with her sensitive single father played by Harry Dean Stanton, persuade her to rise above it and attend the prom anyway. Inspired, Andie sets about creating a special dress out of pink fabric and lace with the finished article kept hidden from the viewer until the end. At the Prom, in true romantic style, Blane stands up to his spoilt friends and wins Andie over. And the dress? Well, unlike the film and the sensational Psychedelic Furs song it is named after, Ringwald is certainly not 'Pretty in Pink'. In fact, the dress is hideous!

Prick Up Your Ears

This 1987 supposed biopic about the life of British playwright Joe Orton featured an exceptionally drawn performance from the then rising star Gary Oldman. The movie really centres on Orton's relationship with Kenneth Halliwell, the lover who was to bludgeon him to death. The movie has an energetic and witty script and handles Orton's promiscuous homosexuality sensitively. Oldman captured Orton's smug yet bewildered reaction to overnight success perfectly whilst Alfred Molina was outstanding as the menacing yet still sympathetic Halliwell.

Prince

Truly one of the world's most prolific and talented musician and songwriters, Prince is a unique entertainer and impossible to slot into any one category. Drawing influence from soul, funk, R&B, rock, New Wave, blues and folk, he is also a prodigious showman constantly reinventing himself. Reported to have written more than one thousand songs, some under pseudonyms he has also written huge hits for other artists including 'Manic Monday' for The Bangles and the haunting 'Nothing Compares 2 U', which launched the career of Sinéad O'Connor.

It is a wonder Prince had a chance to sleep during the 80s given his phenomenal outpouring of work including founding his own recording studio and record label, writing for other bands, self-producing and playing most of the instruments on his recordings. His most notable albums of the 80s are *Dirty Mind*, *Purple Rain*, and *Lovesexy*. Prince's music is also known for its sexual content and explicit lyrics. He holds the dubious accolade of being responsible for the addition of parental

PRINCE

warning labels to recordings deemed unsuitable from minors after morality campaigner Tipper Gore raised merry hell when she heard her 12-year-old daughter listening to 'Darling Nikki'.

Prince been showered with honours and accolades and is the winner of seven Grammy Awards, a Golden Globe and an Oscar for *Purple Rain*.

Prisoner Cell Block H

Based on the popular 70s British drama series *Within These Walls*, this Australian-made copycat became cult viewing in the late 80s. The show followed the lives of a group of women incarcerated in Wentworth Detention Centre and the wardens who guarded them. Unintentionally kitsch, the acting was melodramatic with head honcho Bea ruling the roost and getting the better of the staff. Some of the storylines depicting lesbianism, feminism and violent behaviour were considered quite radical at the time.

Proclaimers, The

With their blond hair and geeky specs, identical twin brothers Charlie and Craig Reid carved out a niche for themselves combining pop, folk, punk and New Wave. Invited by The Housemartins to support them on tour in 1986, the Proclaimers were invited to perform on the influential music show *The Tube* shortly afterwards. Their thick Scottish accents and often political lyrics set them apart from the more frothy pop bands of the mid 80s. Recording their debut album *This is the Story* later that year, readers of the music magazine MNE voted them Best New Act and their single, 'Letter From America', charted at number three. For their second album, 1988's *Sunshine on Leith*, which included their best known track, the exuberant 'I'm Gonna Be (500 Miles)', the brothers embraced country and rock and the title track was adopted as the anthem for their beloved Hibernian football club.

Queen and Freddie Mercury

A truly unique band in terms of musical style and image, Queen are also the only act on earth in which every member has penned a number one hit. By the beginning of the 80s, Mercury and his bandmates Brian May, Roger Taylor and John Deacon had already scored commercial and critical success thanks to the novel, operatic-style content and performance of the monster hit 'Bohemian Rhapsody'. No one doubts the musical talent and songwriting skills of the other members but it was the outlandishly theatrical and flamboyant Mercury who really drove the band and thanks to some truly spectacular live performances, the group was widely regarded as the

FREDDIE MERCURY,
FRONT MAN OF THE
BAND QUEEN.

best live act of the 80s. Queen made five albums in the 80s kicking off with *The Game* in 1980, which contained the hit singles, 'Crazy Little Thing Called Love' and 'Another One Bites the Dust'. The innovative yet distinctive sound of Queen became more popular thanks to their 1984 album *The Works* which included the singles 'Radio Ga Ga' and 'I Want to Break Free', a song enhanced by its promo video which showed Mercury vacuuming a kitsch house whilst dressed as a sluttish woman – but still sporting his trademark handlebar moustache.

In 1985 Queen stole the show at Live Aid. Mercury's enthralling and exhilarating renditions of stadium anthems 'Radio Ga Ga', 'We will Rock You' and 'We Are the Champions' drove the 100,000-strong live audience into an ecstatic frenzy.

A year later and Queen were at it again launching a sell-out tour in support of their latest album *A Kind of Magic*. Unable to book Wembley Stadium for a third night they played Knebworth Park. The show sold out within two hours and more than 120,000 fans packed the park to watch their idols, not knowing that it would prove to be Mercury's final live performance. By the end of the tour, 1 million fans had witnessed the shows – with a record breaking 400,000 in the UK alone. By the late 80s Freddie's gaunt appearance led to speculation that he was suffering with AIDS. Although at first he flatly denied the rumours and produced two further albums, *The Miracle* and *Innuendo*, Mercury prepared a statement from his deathbed in 1991 in which he confirmed that he did have the disease. He died 24 hours later.

Queen's Intruder

On July 7 1982, the Queen, who was sleeping alone, awoke in her bedroom in the Royal Suite of Buckingham Palace to find an unknown man sitting on the foot of her bed. The mentally disturbed intruder Michael Fagan, aged 30, was drinking a bottle of wine that he had earlier removed from her wine cellar and now demanded a chat with the monarch. With extraordinary control and presence of mind the Queen kept calm and waited for a chance to summon help. It occurred when Fagan asked for a cigarette, giving the Queen an opportunity to gain the attention of those who were supposed to be providing her security. Fagan was remanded in custody and charged with theft of a bottle of wine while trespassing.

Incredibly, this wasn't the first breach of Palace security. On another occasion a group of German tourists had managed to gain entry by clambering over a barbed wire fence to camp out in the Queen's garden.

Raging Bull

Raging Bull is a movie of immense power shot in black and white, which gives the streets of New York, filmed in 1980, the feeling of the city decades earlier. Robert De Niro, who won an Academy Award as best actor for his role as world Middleweight champion Jake La Motta, was obsessed by the story and persuaded Martin Scorsese, who had no interest at all in boxing, to direct. The fight sequences are brutal and convincing, but the real triumph of the film was to make a riveting story about a man who is utterly loathsome and has no redeeming characteristics whatsoever.

Raiders of the Lost Ark

Harrison Ford is so linked in people's minds as Indiana Jones, the character who transformed the dry as dust archaeologist into that of treasure-hunting action hero, it is odd to think that the role was originally envisaged for Tom Selleck. George Lucas conceived the idea of making an affectionate homage to the children's Saturday morning serials of the thirties and persuaded Steven Spielberg to direct. Paramount only allowed a relatively modest budget of £20.8 million. Released in 1981, the picture grossed $363 million for the studio, a record only finally broken by *Forrest Gump*. The film moves at a breakneck pace as Indiana Jones, at the bequest of the United States government, seeks the lost Ark of the Covenant to prevent it falling into the hands of Nazi agents. The Ark is the object once carried into battle by the Israelites of the Old Testament that made them invincible. Along the way, Ford is aided by heroine Karen Allen, who had at one point to endure being lowered into a pit carpeted with live snakes. The show is a masterful piece of Hollywood hokum that the whole family really can enjoy.

HARRISON FORD IN *RAIDERS OF THE LOST ARK*.

Rappers

Run-DMC

This trio, consisting of Run, Jam-Master Jay and DMC, hailed from New York's Queens and were partly responsible for hip-hop's elevation from the street to global phenomenon. Known for their entertaining videos, sometimes aggressive rapping and edgy beats, they also distinctively wore bowler hats and thick gold rope chains.

Public Enemy

Possibly the most controversial hip-hop band of the 80s was Public Enemy. Though viewed as ground-breakingly innovative musicians, depending on individual viewpoint they were much criticised or admired for their extreme political message.

Beastie Boys

The first successful white rap group. They developed yet another musical hybrid as they mixed punk and traditional rock with hip-hop and satirical rapping. Their hits included 'No Sleep 'Til Brooklyn' and '(You Gotta)Fight For Your Right (To Party)' Arriving to tour the British Isles in 1987, Beastie Boys Mike D, MCA and Ad-Rock found themselves accused by a hysterical press of corrupting the nation's young and inciting violence. The biggest bone of contention was a giant inflatable penis, used as a prop when performing live on stage!

De La Soul

Unlike other hip-hop acts of the time De La Soul promoted a message of harmony and peace. The 1989 album, *3 Feet High and Rising*, was a critical smash that crossed the bridge separating hip-hop and the more common musical styles of the time. It was unusual, due to a lack of swearing and a focus on love and friendship.

Risky Business

Made in 1983, when Tom Cruise still actually looked young enough to play a teenager, this slick comedy is a hilarious look at how matters can slide into chaos when one mistake leads inevitably to disaster. Tom Cruise plays rich kid, Joel Goodson, whose parents leave him at home in the family mansion when they go away. Joel decides he will hire a hooker to pass the time and Rebecca De Mornay deliciously fills the role of Lana. But Joel wrecks his father's Porsche and to pay for the repairs he decides to set up a brothel in the family home with the assistance of Lana's friends in the same line of work. Things seem to be going famously until Guido, the Killer Pimp, takes exception to Joel stealing his business and decides to teach him a lesson.

TOM CRUISE IN *RISKY BUSINESS.*

Ronald Reagan

Ronald Wilson Reagan was a well-known B-movie actor who became involved in politics as President of the Screen Actors Guild. At first he was a Democrat, but he changed to the Republican Party in 1962 and eventually became Governor of California in 1964. He was elected America's 40th President in 1981 and served two terms. He survived an assassination attempt, and confounded many critics who claimed he had difficulty with the more demanding aspects of his great office. His easy-going charm gradually won over the majority of the country and he ultimately led the USA through the Cold War with the Soviet Union. He was twice married to actresses, first to Jane Wyman and then to Nancy Davis.

Royal Family, The

With two spectacular weddings, four births and a series of scandals, the 80s was a bumper decade for the House of Windsor.

One Prince starred in the largest TV royal wedding of all time, another frolicked with a soft-porn actress, whilst a third quit the Royal Marines in favour of a career in musical theatre.

During the 80s, the press, who had previously been deferential to the Royals, relaxed their attitudes towards printing stories about their personal lives. Suddenly, the most famous family in the world was fair game and the Royal Family started to make headlines for all the wrong reasons.

Charles and Diana.

The fairytale wedding of the heir to the throne (and hitherto confirmed bachelor) and 'Shy Di' took place at St Paul's Cathedral on July 29th' 1981 in front of a TV audience of 750 million. Diana wore a sumptuous Emmanuel-designed ivory gown of antique lace and silk

CHARLES, PRINCE OF WALES, PRINCESS GRACE OF MONACO AND DIANA, PRINCESS OF WALES AT A FUND-RAISING CONCERT.

taffeta with a 25 foot flowing train. Charles wore the full dress uniform of a Naval Commander and the Archbishop of Canterbury led the ceremony. Following the service the bride and groom travelled to Buckingham Palace in the open-topped state landau, driving past hundreds of thousands of well-wishers who had lined the route, many arriving days earlier to secure their spot.

They appeared on the balcony flanked by the rest of the Royal Family, made history when they became the first royal couple to publicly kiss, and the world erupted in a joyous applause. The public's love affair with the Prince and Princess of Wales was further cemented when a year later Diana gave birth to Prince William. Their second child Prince Harry was born two years later but by then rumours had begun to surface that all was not well behind palace doors. The rest, as they say, is history.

Prince Andrew and Sarah Ferguson.

By 1986, with the marriage of Charles and Diana in serious trouble, the Royal Family welcomed the distraction of Andrew's relationship with the girl who appeared to be a breath of fresh air.

Andrew's distinguished service as a naval pilot in the Falklands War had been overshadowed by his many relationships, including one with Koo Stark, an American actress with a dubious past, which had earned him the nickname Randy Andy. It was claimed that the Prince was besotted with the showgirl and intended to marry her but Palace officials and the Queen put a determined stop on it.

So if was with much relief to the rest of the family when he walked down the aisle during another lavish

The King of Pop came to power during the 80s. Michael Jackson in 1981.

Above: One of the UK's most beloved shows, *EastEnders*, began in 1985. Linda Davidson starred as Mary Smith.

Below: Another show that came to epitomise 80s fashion, *Miami Vice* featuring Philip Michael Thomas and Don Johnson.

The famous embrace of Richard Gere and Debra Winger in *An Officer and a Gentleman* (1982).

When Indiana Jones leapt onto our screen in *Raiders of the Lost Ark* (1981), he became one of the most famous 80s heroes.

Movie Posters of the 80s.
Top left: Michael J Fox and Christopher Lloyd in *Back to the Future* (1985).

Bottom right: Glenn Close and Michael Douglas in *Fatal Attraction* (1987).

Clockwise from front: The A-Team, consisting of George Peppard (as Col. John 'Hannibal' Smith), Dirk Benedict (as Lt. Templeton 'Faceman' Peck), Dwight Schultz (as Captain H.M. 'Howling Mad' Murdock), and Mr. T (as Sgt. Bosco 'B.A.' Baracus).

Above: Paul Hogan and Linda Kozlowski in *Crocodile Dundee* (1986).

Below left: Catherine Oxenberg and John Forsythe in *Dallas*, which ran from 1981–1989.

Below right: David Hasselhoff as Michael Knight in *Knight Rider*.

Everyone's favourite 80s TV and music power couple, Kylie Minogue and Jason Donovan. Their *Neighbours* characters, Scott and Charlene, tied the knot in 1987.

ceremony, this time at Westminster Abbey, with Sarah Ferguson, known as Fergie, on 23 July.

The Queen conferred Prince Andrew with a new title just 90 minutes before the ceremony and Andrew and Fergie left the Abbey as the Duke and Duchess of York. Pretty soon however, the public and the press began to criticize Sarah for her weight gain, fashion sense and brash personality, constantly comparing her unfavourably to Diana. Matters were not helped when, after she gave birth to Princess Beatrice in 1988, the Duke and Duchess embarked on a Royal visit to Australia two months later, leaving their baby in England. She has since admitted that her marriage began to break down within a week of the state wedding because of Andrew's naval duties.

Prince Edward

Not an awful lot was written or said about the Queen's third son until the 80s. As the baby of the family, the fresh-faced young Edward was somewhat overshadowed by his older brothers and sister. Nevertheless, controversy was to target the Prince when he was accepted into Cambridge University on the strength of very weak A Level results. But it was his decision to quit the Royal Marines just a third of the way through his year of officer training that attracted the most criticism. Breaking a century-old family tradition of military training, Edward was vilified in the press and it was claimed his father, the Marines' honorary Captain General, was so angry he reduced his son to tears.

Prince Edward was to suffer more humiliation in the press when it was revealed soon after that he was going to join the Really Useful Theatre Company as a production assistant. On his first day of work at the company owned by Andrew Lloyd Webber, Edward was photographed clutching a box of teabags, earning him the nickname of Prince Dogsbody.

In another ill-advised act, to demonstrate his talent for show business and raise money for charity the Prince produced and took part in *It's a Royal Knockout*. Based on the slapstick show from the 70s where competitors, often dressed in ridiculous animal costumes and fancy dress, took part in absurd games that regularly included carrying buckets of water over greasy poles, Edward recruited his sister Princess Anne and the Duchess of York to join him.

Although it raised a lot of money for charity, the show was considered ridiculous by the press and public and rendered Edward a laughing stock.

Princess Anne

Although the only daughter of the Queen continued to work tirelessly for a number of charities, and gave birth to the Queen's second grandchild Zara Phillips in 1981, she was to end the decade by announcing the failure of her marriage to Captain Mark Phillips.

Rubik's Cube

Devised by Erno Rubik, a Hungarian sculptor and architect, the world was confronted by his fiendishly complex invention when it first came to be sold in 1980. It quickly became the best-selling toy of all time. The device consists of a cube, each side of which is divided into six different coloured smaller cubes. The smaller cubes can be pivoted to mix the colours. The trick is to get them all to be the same colour on each side of the larger cube. Hours of frustration are guaranteed.

Rushdie, Salman

When novelist Salman Rushdie published his 1989 novel *The Satanic Verses*, which uses as subject matter the verses that are not included in the Koran, many Muslims were outraged. Rushdie's life was threatened and he had to go into hiding with a police bodyguard.

SALMAN RUSHDIE

S

Sade

The release of successful debut album, *Diamond Life*, saw Sade rise to the pinnacle of fame eventually becoming the most successful female solo artist in British history and earned her an OBE. Beautiful and elegant, Sade's huskily delivered, laid back vocals and slender, designer-clad frame was the antithesis of the fizzy pop of the era. An appearance as a lounge singer in Julian Temple's film version of *Absolute Beginners* was seen by many as the flop movie's only redeeming factor.

Say Anything

Written and directed by Cameron Crowe, this 1989 delightful romantic comedy gave John Cusack a chance to demonstrate his quirky charm when he was cast opposite lovely Ione Skye. That chemical magic that sometimes happens when the right couple are brought together worked in this case, both stars complimented each other's personalities with excellent results.

A fresh story line was explored in which exceptionally clever girl, Diane Court, played by Ione Skye, is attracted to underachiever Lloyd Dobler, played by John Cusack, who is no match for her intellectual abilities. Despite their differing IQ levels love overcomes all obstacles to bring the necessary happy ending.

Scarface

The 1983 version of *Scarface* was dedicated to Howard Hawks and Ben Hecht, who co-wrote the original 1932 version with Hawks directing. Brian De Palma directed this later version, which was produced by Martin Bergman and written by Oliver Stone. Al Pacino starred with Michelle Pfeiffer. The epic saga charts the rise and fall of a Cuban refugee who comes to Miami and fights his way to the top of a multi-million empire founded on the cocaine business. Along the way he acquires Michelle Pfeiffer as his wife, who joins him in a spiral of degradation and addiction before his ultimate death at the hands of rivals.

MICHELLE PFEIFFER AND AL PACINO *SCARFACE*

Scargill, Arthur

Elected President of the National Union of Mineworkers
in 1981, Arthur Scargill was the son of a communist
mineworker and a communist himself, until he joined the
Labour Party in the early sixties. He became the
champion of the hard–left in British politics, but many

members of the Labour Party hierarchy loathed him because they considered his bitter class war tactics made Labour unelectable to the majority of voters. Scargill's driving ambition was to defeat Conservative Prime Minister Margaret Thatcher and hound her from office. He thought his day had come when he called for a strike in 1984. But Margaret Thatcher was ready for him. Stockpiles of coal were high and extra police were drafted from all over the country to confront the picketing miners. After a long and bitter struggle the miners were defeated in 1985 and Arthur Scargill's importance faded as the miners gradually became powerless as practically the whole of the British coal industry ceased to exist.

Selleck, Tom

Thomas William Selleck was born in Detroit, Michigan in 1945 and came from a well-off family; his father was a business executive. In early childhood the family moved to Los Angeles, California, where Selleck grew up and attended the University of Southern California on a basketball scholarship. For some years he worked as a bit player on television and in movies until an occasional part as an irritatingly lucky detective in the Rockford Files lead to his big break. *Magnum P.I.*, in which he starred, was one of the great detective series of the 80s. It charted the cases of Thomas Magnum, the Hawaii-based private eye who always dressed in colourful Hawaiian shirts and a

TOM SELLECK

baseball cap. The excellent scripts and Selleck's charming, easy-going manner made him one of the best light comedians on television, although he was excellent in darker dramatic parts when it proved necessary.

Shakin' Stevens

Known to fans as 'Shaky', the Welsh-born rocker scored three number ones and a further seven top five hits throughout the decade, as well as 30 Top 30 entries. He was one of the most successful chart performers of the 1980s and the 16th highest selling UK music act of all time! Having previously portrayed the young Elvis in the hit west end show of the same name, the photogenic singer was a family favourite with a multi-generational fan base as well as having teen heart throb status.

Sigue Sigue Sputnik

The name is taken from a Moscow street gang and translates into English as 'burn burn satellite'. The band's futuristic-style outrageous image and electronic music gave them a street cred with many young Goths of the era.

Simply Red

In the early 80s, ex art student Mick Hucknall was still with his original Manchester punk group, The Frantic

Elevators. But after they split up in 1984, Hucknall teamed up with manager Elliot Rashman and they began a search for talent to form a new band. Assembling a group of session musicians, they began to be noticed by record companies under the name of Red, adopted because of the colour of Hucknall's hair. When the manager of a club asked what the name of the band was so he could have it printed on a poster, Hucknall replied, 'Red, simply Red.' The promoter misunderstood the remark and billed the band as Simply Red. They liked the accidental title and decided to keep it. The line-up of the rest of the band, which proved to be changeable, was Tony Bowers (bass), Tim Kellett (brass), Sylvan Richardson (guitar), Fritz McIntyre (keyboards), and Chris Joyce (drums).

Citing their influences as being rhythm and blues, pop, soul and new romanticism, they released 'Money's Too Tight' as their first single in 1985 and went on to sell over 50 million albums.

Sinclair, Clive

Difficult to imagine now, but many people thought Sir Clive Sinclair might prove to be Britain's Bill Gates when he began manufacturing calculators, computers and mini TV sets. But his obsession with a strange vehicle he'd developed caused him to be widely mocked. Convinced it would solve Britain's energy problems, traffic congestion and even contribute to the nation's good health, his brainchild was the C5, a curious, low-slung, three-wheeled transporter that was powered by battery assisted pedal power. It provided no protection from the weather and was so slow some experts predicted it would prove to be a road hazard. The invention was ruled to be a tricycle after a drink-driving case and despite backing from Stirling Moss, fewer than 12,000 C5s were sold. It ceased production in 1985 and now the survivors have become collectors' items.

Smith, Mandy

In 1986 16-year-old Mandy Smith found herself at the centre of one of the decade's most shocking scandals. In a newspaper interview, the exquisitely pretty teenager revealed that for the past two and a half years she had been having an affair with 49-year-old Rolling Stone, Bill Wyman. She revealed that the relationship had begun when Smith was just 13 years old, becoming sexual a year later.

Modelling and record contracts followed with Mandy being signed by Stock Aitken and Waterman and having some success as a pop singer. The couple reunited and were married in 1989, though they separated after only a few weeks.

Smiths, The

Formed in 1982 by the famously creative song writing partnership of Morrissey and Johnny Marr, the Manchester band gained legendary status as the voice of 1980s angst-ridden youth. Also featuring Andy Rourke (bass) and Mike Joyce (drums), though 1983 single, 'Hand in Glove', failed to chart, follow up 'What Does it Make' reached number 12. A now-famed appearance on Top of the Pops playing 'This Charming Man', featuring the eccentric Morrissey waving gladioli, and Johnny Marr's exciting opening guitar riffs, introduced the record buying public to a previously unheard alternative sound.

Notorious for their anti-establishment philosophy and fervent vegetarianism, famously documented in number one album, *Meat Is Murder*, they continued to entrance critics and fans until their acrimonious split in 1987.

Space Invaders

In 1980 the Atari 2600 version of Space Invaders became available and quadrupled the arcade video game's sales. Space Invaders was the granddaddy of arcade games. Designed by Tomohiro Nishikado, it was originally manufactured by Taito in Japan. As one of the earliest shooting games it used two-dimensional graphics to add excitement. The aim of the game is for the player to score by destroying hordes of aliens with a laser cannon. It is claimed that Nishikado drew on Star Wars for inspiration when he designed his masterpiece, which has earned him in excess of $500 million to date.

Spandau Ballet

'Gold' was undoubtedly one of the definitive tracks of the 1980s. Spandau Ballet also gave us 'True', the classic last dance track for school discos. Appropriating their name from graffiti seen on a Berlin toilet wall, the good-looking quintet of Tony Hadley, Martin and Gary Kemp, John Keeble and Steve Norman were the self proclaimed 'hippest band in London'. So hip in fact, that in their first year manager Steve Dagger would vet music press

SPANDAU BALLET

wishing to interview the band. If the applicants' dress sense failed to appeal the request was denied. As they also refused to send out demo tapes or invite record companies to 'tease dates' as they called them, it is a miracle they ever hit the big time at all. But they did and with astounding success. The synthesised dance music and Frank Sinatra style vocals paired with a debonair image and razor sharp outfits would further popularise the New Romantic sense of unique dress and new mode of music.

Splash

Starring Tom Hanks, Daryl Hannah and John Candy, this delightful mermaid tale from 1984 was deftly directed by Ron Howard, who saw to it that no one put a foot, or a tail, wrong. Tom Hanks plays a successful New Yorker who can't find love because as a child he had an encounter with a little mermaid girl off Cape Cod. As an adult he returns to the same waters and loses his wallet. Mermaid Daryl Hannah finds it and tracks him home and they fall in love. Out of the water she has two legs, but a persistent mermaid hunter is trailing her, eager to reveal her secret by spraying her with sea water, thus bringing back her tail. There are some great under-water sequences and a series of hilarious scenes in Bloomingdale's department store.

TOM HANKS AND DARYL HANNAH IN *SPLASH*.

Stars on 45

This Dutch novelty act released a medley of classic 1960s hits. Their success ignited a 1980s fad for medley. After scoring a big 1981 hit they released *Best of Stars on 45* a decade later in 1991.

St Elmo's Fire

Joel Schumacher's coming of age drama charts the lives of seven George Town University graduates during the first year of the rest of their lives. St Elmo's is the name of the bar where they congregated in their undergraduate days. Widely considered the defining Brat Pack movie that exemplified the era, it starred Emilio Estevez, Rob Lowe, Demi Moore, Andrew McCarthy, Ally Sheedy, and Judd Nelson.

Steve Strange

Born Steve Harrington, he was the inspiration for the New Romantic movement and the most flamboyant face on the London club scene. The young man from the Welsh valleys was nicknamed the 'Peacock Prince' in reference to his fantastic outfits and spectacular makeup. Pop success with Visage wasn't enough to save him from a battle with heroin addiction, though he did earn a comfortable living as a DJ in the mid to late 80s.

ALLY MOLLOY

ROB LOWE IN *ST ELMO'S FIRE.*

Stone Roses

An alternative rock band from Manchester, their debut album, *Stone Roses*, won critical acclaim and has gone on to be considered one of the greatest British albums of all time. Their reputation for perfectionism earned them accusations of being difficult to deal with. The line-up consisted of vocalist, Ian Brown, guitarist John Squire, bass player Gary 'Mani' Mounfield and drummer Alan 'Reni' Wren. Their musical style, known for the use of guitar with Acid House rhythms, produced one of the significant sounds of the late 80s.

Strawberry Shortcake

Another card illustration for American Greetings that became a TV show, comic book, stationary range and 60 dessert scented toys. Millions of little girls spent their pocket money on Strawberry Shortcake sticker books, clothes and even an Atari video game. The cute little vinyl dolls with luridly coloured hair were named after different dessert treats such as Strawberry Shortcake and Blueberry Pie and they were scented to smell just like them too.

T

Talking Heads

Avant garde rockers Chris Frantz, Tina Weymouth, Jerry Harrison and legendary front man David Byrne were a mainstay of 1980s cool. Byrne's wacky dancing style, distinctive vocals and eccentric lyrics, as well as the band's ahead of their time musical style, makes them one of the most acclaimed acts of the decade.

Talk Talk

The New Wave trio tasted first success as the opening act on Duran Duran's 1982 UK tour. Debut album *The Part's Over* was well received and is now widely considered to epitomise the early 80s synth sound. The ever-evolving style, evident on each successive album ensured massive success at home and abroad.

Tears for Fears

The pop pairing of Roland Orzabal and Curt Smith was made in the early 80s. They specialized in sensitive and moody material and their first album, *The Hurting*, featuring number three hit, 'Mad World', appealed to those sensitive young people who wanted more than in-your-face rock music. The band's lyrics included references to their traumatic childhoods and their emotional history. The record achieved platinum status and spent 65 weeks in the UK charts. In 1985, *Songs From The Big Chair* went straight to number two and remained in the charts for a further year, giving us the never-forgotten singles, 'Shout', 'Head Over Heels' and the 80s anthem, 'Everybody Wants to Rule The World'. Their last album of the decade was 1989's *The Seeds Of Love*, featuring the single of the same name.

Terence Trent D'Arby

Born in Manhattan on 15 March 1962, Terence Trent Howard was the son of Francis Darby, a gospel singer and teacher. He was a keen boxer who received an invitation to attend boxing school in the US Army. Choosing the

University of Central Florida instead, he quit after a year to enlist in the army. Discharged in 1983 for being absent without leave, he stayed in Frankfurt, Germany, where his unit was posted. While in Germany he had some success with a local band called The Touch, releasing the album, *Love On Time* in 1984. Following his later international success, it was reissued as *Early Works*. 1986 saw him relocate in London, briefly play with the band The Bojangles and finally sign a recording deal with Columbia. His debut album, *Introducing The Hardline According to Terence Trent D'Arby*, sold over a million copies in its first three days, and featured his much loved hits, 'Wishing Well' and 'Sign Your Name'. A Grammy for best R&B male vocal performance followed, and his 1989 album, *Neither Fish Nor Flesh*, was bought by over two million fans.

Terminator, The

By 1984, director James Cameron had been touting his script around the Hollywood studios for a couple of years, but only when he cast Arnold Schwarzenegger in the lead role did the project take off. It was a perfect role for a muscle-bound actor with a thick Austrian accent that sounded like a Continental 'speaks your weight' machine. But despite having so little to say (he only had sixteen lines in the whole movie), Arnie made them count and nowadays we can all quote the most famously menacing: 'I'll be back.'

ARNOLD
SCHWARZENEGGER

In the story, a war with the machines threatens the very existence of the human race. Arnie, a cyborg robot, is sent back in time by the machines of the future in order to change the course of history. To do this they have ordered him to kill Sarah Connor, played by Linda Hamilton, because she will become the mother of a child who will grow up to be the saviour of the human race. Humans in the future have learned about the plans of the machines and have sent their own agent into the past to save Sarah Connor from the Terminator.

Thatcher, Margaret

The British political scene throughout the 80s was completely dominated by Margaret Thatcher, who was elected Conservative Prime Minister in 1979 and stayed at Number 10 until she was overthrown by members of her own party in 1990. The daughter of a grocer from Grantham in Lincolnshire, she was the first woman to become Prime Minister and initially had to battle opponents in her own cabinet who thought her confrontational style would destroy the social fabric of the country. Constantly supported by her husband Denis, who became an affectionately comical figure in the eyes of the nation, she ordered the invasion of the Falkland Islands when Argentinean Forces occupied them in 1982. When the British Army proved victorious she saw her popularity soar. Despite the hatred she engendered in the

MARGARET
THATCHER

political left, she defeated Arthur Scargill in the miner's strike of 1984/85. She narrowly survived the IRA bombing of the Grand Hotel Brighton and was often known as the Iron Lady.

Thompson Twins

Named after the characters in the comic strip *The Adventures of Tintin*, the Thompson Twins were actually a trio. Their real names were Tom Bailey, Alannah Currie, and Joe Leeway. They broke into the singles charts in 1983 with 'Lies', and reached international success at the end of that year with their best-loved single, 'Hold Me Now'. A further hit was 'Doctor, Doctor'. Leeway left in 1986, while Bailey and Currie had a baby and went to write Debbie Harry's 1989 comeback single, 'I Want That Man'.

Tiffany

Tiffany Renee Darwish was born in California on 2 October 1971. The teeny popstrel's name was shortened to just 'Tiffany' and she was cleverly prompted by her public relations company into giving free concerts in shopping malls across America and Europe. Her 1987 hit, 'I Think We're Alone Now', reached the number one spot on both sides of the Atlantic. Then she faded from the scene.

Tina Turner

Born Anna Mae Bullock on 26 November 1939 in Nutbush, Tennessee, Tina Turner has been dubbed the Queen of Rock 'n' Roll. She is the daughter of Floyd Richard Bullock, a farm and factory worker and a Baptist deacon. Tina claims Native American ancestry as well as African-American and European heritage.

Tina met Ike Turner, the man who was to be her mentor, husband and Svengali-like controller, in the late fifties. Eventually they formed a professional partnership

TINA TURNER

and achieved considerable success over the years until
Tina could no longer bear to submit to his domination.
Penniless, she ran away from the marriage and in the 80s
began to forge another hugely successful career as a solo
artist. As one of the world's most popular entertainers,
Tina has sold more concert tickets than any other artist
and taken several film roles. Rolling Stone Magazine
called her, '...one of the greatest singers of all time',

and even Prince Charles said '…she has the best legs in the world.'

Tootsie

Feminism was the big issue when the hit comedy *Tootsie* was released in 1982, but most of the points the film made are woven into the plot with such humour you never get the feeling you're being preached at. Dustin Hoffman is outstanding and absolutely believable as the actor who can't get parts because he's so temperamental to work with, until he poses as a woman to land a role in a daytime TV soap opera. Throwing himself wholeheartedly into the part he is soon in touch with his feminine side, but he falls for his co-star, Jessica Lange, which obviously causes difficulties. A strong supporting cast make the movie a genuinely feel good experience.

Top Gun

Sometimes referred to as 'Top Grin' by movie buffs because of the star's trademark smile, this 1986, chrome-plated, carefully crafted, star-making vehicle sent Tom Cruise's career into orbit. In it he plays Lt Pete 'Maverick' Mitchell, a rebellious navy pilot who is hell bent on coming out as top of the class in the selection of best pilot in gunnery school and seducing the beautiful Kelly McGillis, Charlotte 'Charlie' Blackwood. There's a subplot dealing with Maverick's successful attempt to clear his father's reputation as a disgraced pilot, but the film was directed by Tony Scott in order to enjoy the sheer glamour of it all, rather than bothering with the flimsy plot. Another plus was the movie's theme song, 'Take My Breath Away', which won an Oscar. Everybody loved the film, including the US Navy, who set up recruitment sites outside American cinemas to beguile youths still dreaming of such glory to sign up as they left the movie houses.

T'Pau

Borrowing their name from a Star Trek character, T'Pau had a string of top ten hits including 'Heart and Soul' and 'China in Your Hands' which was Number one in the UK for five weeks in 1987. Led by flame-haired singer/songwriter Carol Decker they stayed in the mainstream until the decade's close.

Transvision Vamp

Formed in 1986 in the English seaside town of Brighton, the rock group quickly became media favourites, thanks to singer Wendy James's raunchy on-stage antics. Their biggest success in 1989 was the single 'Baby I Don't Care', from their number one hit album, *Velveteen*. They stayed in the charts for twenty-six weeks but failed to build on their success in the years that followed.

Trivial Pursuit

When two Canadian journalists, Scott Abbott and Chris Haney, discovered that some of the pieces were missing from their Scrabble set, so they decided to invent their own board game instead, and Trivial Pursuit was born. Launched in 1982, the game flashed around the world and made the journalists multi millionaires. To play the game, contestants must answer questions read aloud on entertainment, geography, history, sport and leisure, science and nature, and art and literature. Variations of the game are produced that appeal to different participants.

Tube, The

First shown on Channel 4 in November 1982, *The Tube* was a ground breaking music programme that show-cased many performers who would go on to even greater success. Presented by Paula Yates, Jules Holland and Muriel Gray, was essential viewing for the era's younger generation. During the fifth series the often controversial show gained even greater infamy when Jools Holland entreated the tea-time audience to, 'Be there, or be ungroovy F★★★★★s.' The national scandal that ensued saw the show taken off air for three weeks. The show was pilloried in the press and Holland was given a severe reprimand.

UB40

The British reggae band that hailed from Birmingham took their name from a card issued to the unemployed. Coming to prominence in 1980, they went on to sell 70 million records worldwide. They were discovered by Chrissie Hynde of The Pretenders, who first heard them playing in a pub. Their earlier songs dealt with the political and social issues of the time, an example being the 1981 single 'One in Ten' which referenced the percentage of unemployed in Britain at the time. They later had a number one hit in several countries with their cover of Neil Diamond's ode to lost love, 'Red, Red Wine'.

Ullman, Tracey

Born 30 December 1959 in Slough, Berkshire, Tracey Ullman attended the Italia Conti stage school after a recommendation from the headmaster of her previous school. Starting as a dancer, Tracey worked in West End musicals such as *The Rocky Horror Show* and *Grease*. She first found fame in the television sketch shows, *A Kick Up The Eighties*, and *Three Of A Kind*. Recognised as a gifted comedienne and impersonator she also pursued a successful career as a singer. In 1983 she signed with Punk label Stiff Records and made the well-received album, *You Broke My Heart In Seventeen Places*. It consisted mostly of cover versions and previous hits, including her UK Number two and US top ten hit, 'They Don't Know'. She also covered the old Doris Day number, 'Move Over Darling' and the Madness hit, 'My Girl', which she altered to 'My Guy' – and the then Labour leader Neil Kinnock appeared with her in the video.

Ultravox

One of the foremost bands of the New Romantic movement, the group was fronted by Scot Midge Ure. They had greatest success with the 1981 album and single, *Vienna*. The video was heavily influenced by the classic black and white movie, *The Third Man*, which was filmed in London and the Austrian capital. The famous theatre scene was shot in a North London Bingo Hall.

Untouchables, The

Brian De Palma directed the 1987 movie with a taunt screenplay by David Mamet. It starred Kevin Costner as Elliot Ness, the man appointed by the US government to bring down Al Capone and the rest of the prohibition bootleggers who flouted the law and turned American cities into shooting ranges. Sean Connery won an Oscar for his role as an old time incorruptible cop and Robert De Niro was chilling in the role of the psychopathic Al Capone. For film buffs, a brilliantly choreographed gun battle that takes place on the stairway of a railway station is modelled on an iconic scene from the legendary Russian director Sergei Eisenstein's epic silent film, *Battleship Potemkin*.

V

Valley Girl

Strictly for the teenage market, this 1983 high school romantic comedy saw Nicolas Cage drop his family name of Coppola to star as Randy opposite Deborah Foreman as Julie Richman. Martha Coolidge made her debut as a director and the tiny budget of $350,000 saw it gross over $17,000,000.

The writers, Wayne Crawford and Andrew Lane, were reputed to have finished the script in ten days, which isn't surprising when they based it loosely on Shakespeare's *Romeo and Juliet*.

NICOLAS CAGE IN *VALLEY GIRL*.

Vangelis

A passage of music that has the power to instantly evoke memories is the theme from *Chariots of Fire*. The first few bars summon up one of the most heart-lifting movie images from the 80s and once again we see those young British Olympic contestants running along a Yorkshire beach. Vangelis is the professional name of the Greek composer Evangelos Papathanassiou, who wrote the music. He also composed the equally memorable theme for the cult science fiction movie *Blade Runner*.

View to a Kill, A

As the fourteenth James Bond adventure to be filmed, this 1985 movie was the seventh and last outing for Roger Moore as Bond. Ably directed by John Glenn, the music was composed by John Barry and performed by Duran Duran. Christopher Walken made an excellent villain and Tanya Roberts and the startling Grace Jones supplied the always-important female ingredients. The plot was the usual formula: super villain threatens the world, 007 destroys villain and gets the girl.

VHS Video

Another wonder of the electronics age that became available to the mass market by the 80s was the VHS (Home Video System), courtesy, once again, of the Japanese.

ROGER MOORE AS BOND IN *A VIEW TO KILL*.

Developed by JCV (Victor Company of Japan) it finally won out against close competition from Betamax. Simple to use, VHS allowed people the chance to be free of the constrictions of broadcasted programmes. From now on the public could watch recordings they had made from their own television sets, or they could buy or hire cassettes in the high street.

Vintage Rockers

Paul McCartney

As the last Beatle to stay on the road and play venues before the public, Paul McCartney was still performing throughout the 80s, even though his band, Wings, broke up in 1981.

Rod Stewart

The early 80s were a slow time for Rod Stewart, but in 1985, at the Rock in Rio concert in Rio de Janeiro, he performed before a wildly enthusiastic audience of over 100,000 during a storm. Stewart said, 'It was like winning the world soccer championship.' The following year he released 'Every Beat Of My Heart', which reached Number two and his career took off again.

Mick Jagger and The Rolling Stones

In the 80s, friction in the band between Mick Jagger and Keith Richards saw Jagger performing more as a solo artist. He released his first solo album, *She's The Boss*, in 1985, and the single from it, 'Just Another Night', became a top ten hit. The same year he also reached Number one with 'Dancing in the Streets', which he made with David Bowie.

David Bowie

In 1980 Bowie began the decade by starring on Broadway for three months in the play *The Elephant Man*. In 1983 he produced his first outstanding commercial hit with the album *Let's Dance*. The title track went on to be Number one in Britain and America. Bowie's final album of the 80s was in 1987 with *Never Let Me Down*. He later described it as, 'My nadir... an awful album.'

Visage

Steve Strange and Rusty Egan's band, Visage, briefly featured a pre-Ultravox Midge Ure. The dandyish club promoters were also founders of the New Romantic scene and recorded the musical movement's principal single and video, 'Fade To Grey'. The single was a worldwide smash hit. The Edwardian influenced garb, including knickerbockers and berets, would filter from high fashion into the mainstream, while the beautiful and ever-changing make-up sported by Strange was the result of an attempt to create something very visual on a low budget.

Voice of the Beehive

Formed in 1986 in London by two Californian sisters, Tracy Bryn and Melissa Brooke, Voice of the Beehive was a popular alternative band. Other members included Mike Jones, guitar, Martin Brett, bass, and Madness drummer Woody Woodgate. Tracy played guitar and sang with her sister.

Walkman, The

Akio Morita, the co-chairman of Sony, wanted a way to listen to opera on his frequent long-haul trips across the Pacific so he put his problem to Nabutoshi Kihara, an audio engineer. Kihara came up with the solution in 1978 and by the 80s anyone who was anyone had a Walkman. Morita hated the name and wanted to change it but by then vast amounts of money had gone into marketing and promotion, so he was stuck with it. Other countries called it something different, it was the Soundabout in the USA, Freestyle in Sweden and Stowaway in Britain, but the name Walkman stuck in people's minds.

Wall Street

Directed by Oliver Stone, who also co-wrote the script with Stanley Weiser, the 1987 movie *Wall Street* was a searing attack on the greed and unscrupulous moral values of some American business tycoons. Michael Douglas, who won the Oscar for best actor, plays the role of Gordon Gekko, the anti-hero, and a man who will go to any lengths to increase his fortune. One of the people he destroys in the process is Charlie Sheen, as Bud Fox, an ambitious entrant into Wall Street, who comes from a

MICHAEL DOUGLAS
IN *WALL STREET*.

working class background. Martin Sheen plays the role of Charlie Sheen's father, a decent mechanic who despises the way his son earns a living. One of the most memorable lines of the movie is Gordon Gekko's defence of his business methods to shareholders: Greed is good.'

Wargames

This morality lesson for teenage hackers was made in 1983 and saw Matthew Broderick playing David Lightman, a computer whiz kid who thinks he's hacked into a new super computer game but in fact has entered the electronic mind that will take over and direct future nuclear warfare in the event of an attack on the USA. Having triggered the sequence of events that will set about the destruction of the planet, he has only one hope. While being pursued by the secret service he must locate the retired scientist who devised the doomsday machine and see if the can find a way to turn off the machine before the coming Russian attack destroys the world.

We Are The World

The United States' answer to Live Aid's 'Do They Know It's Christmas?', 'We Are The World' was, written by Lionel Richie and Michael Jackson and produced by the legendary Quincy Jones and recorded by super-group USA For Africa in 1985. Like its predecessor, it was a worldwide

SUPER-GROUP USA FOR AFRICA. CAN YOU SPOT TINA TURNER, MICHAEL JACKSON, STEVIE WONDER AND DIANA ROSS?

commercial success, becoming the fastest selling American pop single in history. 'We Are The World' featured:

Lead vocalists:

Lionel Richie, Stevie Wonder, Paul Simon, Kenny Rogers, James Ingram, Tina Turner, Billy Joel, Michael Jackson, Diana Ross, Dionne Warwick, Willie Nelson, Al Jarreau, Bruce Springsteen, Kenny Loggins, Steve Perry, Daryl Hall, Huey Lewis, Cyndi Lauper, Kim Carnes, Bob Dylan and Ray Charles.

Chorus:

Dan Aykroyd, Harry Belafonte, Lindsey Buckingham, Mario Cipollina, Johnny Colla, Sheila E., Bob Geldof, Bill Gibson, Chris Hayes, Sean Hopper, Jackie Jackson, La Toya, Marlon Jackson, Randy Jackson, Tito Jackson, Waylon Jennings, Bette Midler, John Oates, Jeffrey Osborne, Anita Pointer, Ruth Pointer, and Smoky Robinson.

Weird Science

The original idea for this 1985 movie a short story called *Made in the Future* that first appeared in a copy of *Weird Science*, a comic from the fifties. The movie was written and directed by John Hughes as the dream fulfilment wish of every teenage boy who is not having much success with girls. The plot involves two nerdy types, played by Anthony Michael Hall and Ilan Mitchell-Smith, who are humiliated by the girls at their high school. After an experiment with a computer they succeed in creating an electronic Frankenstein's monster. Only their monster is the fabulously sexy Kelly LeBrock, who sets out to show the boys what a good time really is.

Weller, Paul

Singer and songwriter Paul Weller was born 25 May 1958. After his successful band, The Jam, split in 1982, Weller went on a year later to form The Style Council. The line-up included Mick Talbot, keyboard, drummer Steve White, and Weller's soon-to-be-wife, vocalist Dee C. Lee. In a change from Weller's previous Mod revival sound with The Jam, The Style Council's tracks were heavily influenced by funk and soul. Hit records included, 'Long Hot Summer', 'Shout To the Top', 'Walls Came Tumbling Down', and 'You're The Best Thing'. Projecting themselves with a cool, well-dressed image, the band opened the gates to a breakaway from the punky, outlandish look that had previously dominated popular culture.

Whitbread, Fatima

Fatima had a tragic early childhood having been abandoned by her Turkish Cypriot mother, but eventually she was adopted by the Whitbread family and went on to become, as a javelin thrower, one of Britain's most famous and successful athletes. She won a string of medals and broke the world record in the qualifying round of the 1986 European Championships with a throw of 77.44m. She was much loved in Britain for her victory wiggle.

Who framed Roger Rabbit?

Based on the novel *Who Censored Roger Rabbit*, Roger Zemeckis directed the unlikely hit movie of 1988. Set in a surreal world where human beings exist side by side with the cartoon characters inhabiting Toon Town, the plot is an affectionate homage to the hard-boiled detective stories of the thirties and forties. The story concerns Roger Rabbit, a major star of cartoon films, being framed for murder. He hires human detective Eddie Valiant, played by Bob Hoskins, to get him off the hook. By employing their technical skills the studio special effects wizards seamlessly melded cartoon characters with human beings so that the audience was able to suspend their disbelief and actually imagine that Bob Hoskins' new best buddy is actually a cartoon creation. In 2009, Roger's beautiful cartoon wife, Jessica, was selected the sexiest animated character ever by *Empire* magazine.

Wilde, Kim

Born Kim Smith in the west London suburb of Chiswick, Kim Wilde is the daughter of fifties Rock 'n' Roll star

Marty Wilde (real name Reginald Smith). Her mother, Joyce Baker, was also a singer and dancer. Kim's first big hit was in 1981, when she released 'Kids in America', but made scant progress in the USA until her record, 'You Keep Me Hangin' On' hit the top of the charts. As well as being a television presenter and author, she also pursued an alternative career as a gardener.

Willcox, Toyah

The pint-sized punk princess first appeared in late 70s cult movies, *Jubilee* and *Quadrophenia*. Willcox was classically trained as an actress, yet became better known in the 80s for her singing career. Her first hit, 'It's A Mystery', and the subsequent 'I Want To Be Free', were successful enough to see her voted Best Female Singer at the 1982 British Rock and Pop Awards. Her ever-changing hair colour, often a blend of pink, purple, blonde and black, and her artistically applied fantasy make-up led to the launch of a successful make-up range aimed at the teenage market.

Xmas Number Ones

1980: St Winifred's School Choir had the nation humming 'There's No one Quite Like Grandma'.

1981: The Human League gave us 'Don't You Want Me?'

1982: Renee and Renato were on top with 'Save Your Love'.

1983: The Flying Pickets scored with 'Only You'.

1984: Band Aid made it with 'Do They Know It's Christmas?'.

1985: Shakin' Stevens rocked back with 'Merry Christmas Everyone'.

1986: Jackie Wilson looked back in time to find 'Reet Petite'.

1987: Pet Shop Boys with the old Elvis favourite 'You Were Always On My Mind'.

1988: Cliff Richard proved he still had it in him with 'Mistletoe and Wine'.

1989: Band Aid II had another go at 'Do They Know It's Christmas?'.

Yates, Paula

The 80s saw the rapid expansion of 'Celebrity Culture', where being famous was financially rewarding to an individual no matter how limited their talents. No one demonstrated this more forcefully than Paula Yates, who until she landed the job of co-presenter alongside Jools Holland on the Channel 4 pop music programme, *The Tube*, was best known to the public as the partner to Bob Geldof of the Boomtown Rats, with whom she had three daughters. She also tried her hand as a pop singer by recording Nancy Sinatra's old hit, 'These Boots Were Made for Walking', but musical success eluded her.

In her relentless drive for publicity Paula Yates had

already posed naked for Penthouse Magazine and tried her hand as a music journalist, having also written a column for the Record Mirror entitled 'Natural Blonde'.

Born in Colwyn Bay, North Wales, she had been brought up in an eccentric show business family. Her mother, who wrote erotic novels, was an ex-dancer and actress who had used two stage names: Heller Toren and Helene Thornton. Married to Jess Yates, who was known as the Bishop in show business circles, he presented the religious TV programme *Stars on Sunday*. Paula had always believed Jess Yates to be her father, but in later life it was revealed that the prominent show business figure, Hughie Green, was actually her biological parent.

Yazoo

The synth-pop duo was known by the name Yaz in the United States. Formed in 1981 by Depeche Mode songwriter Vince Clarke and half-French singer Alison Moyet, their debut single, 'Only You', got to number two in the charts followed by another top five hit, 'Don't Go'. They split in 1983, with Moyet going on to a highly acclaimed solo career and Clarke finding equal success with new band, Erasure.

Yorkshire Ripper, The

On 5 January 1981, a long distance lorry driver called Peter Sutcliffe was charged with murdering Jacqueline Hill, a Leeds student, whose body had been discovered two months earlier. So, one of Britain's most famous murder hunts ended after six years, along with a botched investigation that broke the reputation of George Oldfield, the Assistant Chief Constable in charge of the case.

Sutcliffe killed thirteen women and created an atmosphere of terror that caused near panic in the population of the North of England. Despite interviewing Sutcliffe on several occasions, and possessing a photo-fit portrait of the wanted man that bore a remarkable resemblance to the lorry driver, Oldfield stuck stubbornly to his theory that they were looking for another man. A hoaxer had sent letters and tape recordings claiming to be the murderer and personally taunting Oldfield. Because the voice on the tapes had a Geordie accent Oldfield was convinced the guilty man was from the Wearside district of Country Durham, and that's where he concentrated police efforts. In the end, sheer luck and the sharpness of a police constable saw Sutcliffe caught. Police on a routine patrol questioned Sutcliffe because he was badly parked. At the time a prostitute, Olivia Reivers, who would certainly have been his fourteenth victim, accompanied him. Sutcliffe asked if he could relieve himself while the police were questioning him and he walked some distance from the car. A radio check revealed that Sutcliffe's vehicle had false number plates and he was taken him to the police station for further questioning.

In custody, Sutcliffe once more asked to use a toilet. One of the policemen who had just detained him became suspicious and returned to where they had stopped him earlier. He searched the ground near where Sutcliffe had appeared to have relieved himself and discovered a knife, a hammer and a length of rope. In the police station they found yet another knife concealed in the cistern of the toilet where Sutcliffe had relieved himself for the second time. He went to trial on May 22 1981 and was found guilty and sentenced to life imprisonment.

Young Ones, The

First broadcast in 1982, the brilliant blend of surreal sit-com and slapstick humour made the show an instant hit and captivated a devoted audience. Born out of the new wave of British comedy, it was created by Rik Mayall, Ben Elton, and Lise Mayer with contributions from Alexei Sayle. The storyline concerned four young men who occupy a grotty house owned by, landlord Jerzy Balowski (Alexei Sayle). Students at Scumbag College, located somewhere in London, the four heroes are Vyvyan, a punk metal fan, played by Adrian Edmondson, the tiresome, would-be anarchist Rick, played by Rik Mayall, Nigel Planer as the gentle, anguished hippie, Neil, and the strangely mysterious mod, Mike, played by Christopher

NIGEL PLANER AS NEIL PYE IN *THE YOUNG ONES*.

Ryan. To show the comic interplay of stereotypes from such differing youth tribes was an inspired decision, as it allowed each of those parodied segments to laugh at each other's foibles as well as their own.

Young, Paul

The white soul singer started his musical career as a bass guitarist. That all changed when he was signed as a solo performer by CBS records. His first single, 'Love Of The Common People', had some UK success, but it was his cover of the Marvin Gaye classic, 'Wherever I Lay My Hat (That's My Home)', which confirmed his heartthrob pop star status. His next release, 'Come Back And Stay', raised him to international star status, though success in America was temporarily thwarted when he strained his vocal cords during his first US tour in 1984, which left him unable to sing for a year.

Youth Tribes

Goths

Sporting all-black garb, with lipstick, nail varnish and hair to match, the Goths were kids with something to say…they just didn't like talking much, 'cos they were moody teenagers…right? Their heroes were The Cure and Siouxsie and the Banshees.

Psychobilly

The Psychobilly bands played a hybrid of punk and 1960s rockabilly. They had Mohawk style quiffs that were often bleached. Dressed like 1950s rock 'n' rollers who had discovered punk, the Psychobilly had no political affiliations (unusual for the 1980s) and gigs were promoted as 'politics-free zones' – they were strictly for dancing.

Casuals

The pre-chav casual was working class, liked football and left school at 16. They loved labels, the more expensive the better. Burberry was a big favourite along with Farah trousers and Pringle jumpers. Girls wore box pleated skirts and loads of gold jewellery, particularly sovereign rings and rope chains.

Skins

There was a skinhead revival in the 1980s. Unlike their 1960s counterparts who were greatly influenced by West Indian culture, many revivalist Skins were unpleasant racist thugs. They had shaved heads, wore Ben Sherman or Fred Perry shirts, Sta-Prest trousers or Levis, braces and Doc Martens. Girls wore mini skirts, Fred Perry shirts with fishnet tights and monkey boots. Hair was short on the crown with a feather fringe at front, sides and back. They hated the Mods.

Mods

Back came the Mods with another 80s revival. Scooters, Parkas, sharp haircuts and suits. They still loved Northern Soul and The Who, as well as new band The Specials. They hated the Skinheads.

Trendies or New Beats

Strictly retro, though some modern bands like The Smiths and Lloyd Cole and the Commotions were acceptable listening. They read Allen Ginsberg, J. D. Salinger and wore polo necks with long black overcoats. Both sexes loved paisley shirts; the girls would secure the collar with diamante brooches.

Yuppies

The term 'yuppie' is though to have come into the language from America where it was first published in an article for a Chicago magazine by Dan Rottenburg. Used as an acronym for Young Upwardly-mobile Professional or Young Urban Professional, 'yuppie' became shorthand for the affluent middle class professionals in their late twenties and early thirties. At first it was merely a convenient handle for a socio-economic group but it quickly evolved into a term of abuse or contempt.

Z

Zodiac Mindwarp and The Love Reaction

The hard rock group had their heyday in the mid to late 80s as the creation of graphic artist, Mark Manning, when he assumed the alter ego of hardcore rocker, Zodiac Mindwarp. Their offensive, misogynistic lyrics were actually intended as an ironic parody of other hard rock bands popular at the time.

ZX Spectrum

Another brainchild from Sir Clive Sinclair was the ZX Spectrum, Britain's first affordable home computer. It came in two versions, the more expensive being the 48

KB machine, which sold for £175. The other cheaper version was the 16KB that cost £125. The ZX Spectrum, which was sold in kit form, proved to be an astonishing success. With expected monthly sales of 1,000, they actually sold at a rate of 200,000 a month. Sinclair Research went on to release two further spectrum models before Amstrad bought the brand in 1986.

ZZ Top

The trio from Texas were known as much for their chest length beards, black leather garb and ever present sunglasses, as their music. They are best remembered for their 1984 album, *Eliminator*, which included the singles 'Give Me All Your Loving' and 'Legs'.

ZZ TOP'S *ELIMINATOR* ALBUM COVER.